THE PSYCHOLOGY OF ADDICTION

When does a harmless habit become an addiction? Why do only some of us get addicted? What can make recovery possible?

The Psychology of Addiction is a fascinating introduction to the psychological issues surrounding addiction and the impact they have on social policy, recovery and an addict's everyday life. The book focuses on drug and alcohol addiction and tackles topics such as whether drug use always leads to addiction and the importance of social networks to recovery. It also looks at how people can become addicted to activities like gambling, gaming and sex.

In a society that still stigmatises addiction *The Psychology of Addiction* emphasises the importance of compassion, and provides a sensitive insight to anyone with experience of addiction.

Jenny Svanberg is a Consultant Clinical Psychologist. She has extensive clinical experience working alongside people with drug and alcohol addiction.

THE PSYCHOLOGY OF EVERYTHING

The Psychology of Everything is a series of books which debunk the myths and pseudo-science surrounding some of life's biggest questions.

The series explores the hidden psychological factors that drive us, from our sub-conscious desires and aversions, to the innate social instincts handed to us across the generations. Accessible, informative, and always intriguing, each book is written by an expert in the field, examining how research-based knowledge compares with popular wisdom, and illustrating the potential of psychology to enrich our understanding of humanity and modern life.

Applying a psychological lens to an array of topics and contemporary concerns – from sex to addiction to conspiracy theories – *The Psychology of Everything* will make you look at everything in a new way.

Titles in the series:

The Psychology of Grief
Richard Gross

The Psychology of Sex
Meg-John Barker

The Psychology of Dieting
Jane Ogden

The Psychology of Performance
Stewart T. Cotterill

The Psychology of Trust
Ken J. Rotenberg

The Psychology of Working Life
Toon Taris

The Psychology of Conspiracy Theories
Jan-Willem van Prooijen

The Psychology of Addiction
Jenny Svanberg

The Psychology of Fashion
Carolyn Mair

The Psychology of Gardening
Harriet Gross

The Psychology of Gender
Gary W. Wood

For further information about this series please visit www.thepsychologyofeverything.co.uk

THE PSYCHOLOGY OF ADDICTION

JENNY SVANBERG

LONDON AND NEW YORK

First published 2018
by Routledge
2 Park Square, Milton Park, Abingdon, Oxon OX14 4RN

and by Routledge
605 Third Avenue, New York, NY 10017

Routledge is an imprint of the Taylor & Francis Group, an informa business

British Library Cataloguing-in-Publication Data
A catalogue record for this book is available from the British Library

Library of Congress Cataloging-in-Publication Data
A catalog record for this book has been requested

ISBN: 978-1-138-20727-1 (hbk)
ISBN: 978-1-138-20728-8 (pbk)
ISBN: 978-1-315-46265-3 (ebk)

Typeset in Joanna
by Apex CoVantage, LLC

For Forth Valley Recovery Community, and the 'Dream Team', for the chats, cake and inspiration.

CONTENTS

ACKNOWLEDGEMENTS

Thanks to Lucy Kennedy at Psychology Press for the opportunity, and to those who read early drafts of the book. I am very grateful for your advice and encouragement. There are many people who provided the inspiration and motivation to write this, not all of whom I can name, but I hope you know who you are. Particular thanks to Sean McCann, Katy Sinclair, Grant Brand, Calum Blair, Flip Aveyard, Rachel Crespo-Bonney and the Svanbergs, and apologies to anyone I've missed. All the errors are still mine.

Thanks most of all to the staff and service users of Glasgow Addiction Service and Forth Valley Substance Misuse Service for everything you taught me. It's a long road, but there's always hope.

And thanks last but not least, to Lance.

INTRODUCTION

There are many stories told about addiction and most of them disagree with each other. Is addiction a disease, or a moral weakness? Is it the inevitable consequence of drug use, or a choice? If it's about the drugs, what about addictions to gambling, sex, shopping, exercise, video games, food, wealth, power? Are they real addictions too? If it's about the drugs, why doesn't everyone who uses drugs get hooked? Do some people just have addictive personalities? Whatever it is, there is no doubt that it is a significant problem. Although drug use is falling, drug-induced deaths in the UK are at their highest level since records began, three times higher than the European average (EMCDDA, 2017b). Drug overdose is the number one cause of accidental death in the US (CDC, 2011), and is continuing to rise. America is not only said to be in the grip of a prescription opiate epidemic, but also an obesity epidemic influenced by addiction to high-fat foods. The UK isn't far behind, with the highest rates of obesity in Western Europe (AMRC, 2013). Problematic drug and alcohol use can be just as damaging as addictive use. About half of all violent assaults are alcohol related, and one in four of our young men who die between the ages of 16 and 24 die as a result of alcohol-related causes (PHE, 2014). The costs of addiction and problematic substance use are well-documented, but the personal costs and tragedies within these statistics are incalculable. The billions of pounds and dollars that have been spent on preventing and treating addiction and harmful drug and alcohol use do not seem to be working, and you have to wonder if it's because we are getting it seriously wrong.

This book is an attempt to address some of the questions and conflicting beliefs around addiction and addictive behaviours, and there are a few themes that will be explored throughout the chapters. Addiction is not a moral failing or a choice. The disease (or medical) model, which understands addiction as a brain disease influenced by genetic vulnerability, is most widely known, but has some significant flaws. Arguably, it is too limiting to understand addiction as a disease, which Chapter 1 will explore in more detail. Drug use is not the same as drug addiction, and this distinction is true of other addictive behaviours. Addictive behaviours are at the extreme end of a spectrum that we all sit on; they follow the same processes that we all use to identify and pursue things that we see as important to our survival. With addiction, these habits become deeply entrenched and overvalued, so that they begin to push out other, previously important parts of life. This is true no matter the object of addiction, whether drugs, alcohol, computer games or work. Our brains are designed to create habits, and the most entrenched habits are those that serve fundamental emotional needs: for belonging, for safety and security, for control and autonomy, for relief of overwhelming pain. Addiction tricks people by sending them after things that can never meet their needs in the long run, like the 'hungry ghosts' of Tibetan Buddhism: beings with huge empty bellies, but mouths the size of pinpricks, so that no matter what they eat, they can never be satisfied. The author and physician Gabor Maté described this as "the domain of addiction, where we constantly seek something outside ourselves to curb an insatiable yearning for relief or fulfilment" (2010, p. 1). We all have some capacity to develop addictive behaviours, and certain factors in our biology, psychology and social environment make this more or less likely at different times in our lives. Recovery (and most people do recover from all kinds of addictive behaviours, usually without treatment) is about learning how to harness those tricky brain processes, and finding healthier and more sustainable ways of meeting those needs. This often involves finding safe and compassionate relationships, connecting, feeling accepted and understood. In order to heal old wounds, society must take a compassionate approach to enable recovery, and learn to nourish the hungry ghosts among us.

This book has been informed by my experience working as a clinical psychologist for specialist community drug and alcohol addiction teams in Scotland. When I started, I was mostly naïve about addiction; most of my awareness came from my training, from the way my friends and family thought about drug and alcohol use, as well as from the media – knowledge from books, rather than experience, as some service users would later tell me. These lessons did not equip me for the work ahead, with people who would express a desperate wish to change during sessions, then go back around the same old cycles as soon as they left, or with those who struggled to know what they thought or felt much of the time, and just seemed to react from moment to moment without planning, and in spite of the sometimes terrible consequences of which they were all too aware. I heard staff describing the need for people to 'hit rock bottom' before they would be able to change, and wondered where 'bottom' was, for people who had already endured so much. I would read old psychiatric records with labels for the same person ranging from 'bipolar disorder' to 'anxiety and depression' to 'borderline personality disorder' – and on one occasion 'inadequate personality disorder', a label which has thankfully been removed from the diagnostic manuals. If anything, this confusion illustrated the limits of a medical, or diagnostic, model for describing complex mental health difficulties, particularly when they occur alongside addictive behaviours. I realised how much of the floating stigma about addiction I had absorbed: why weren't these people trying harder to change? Maybe they weren't motivated enough. Maybe it was me and I was just terrible at my job. Many of the staff I worked with had been in the service for years and had seen several generations of the same families coming through the doors. You can imagine what that does for your hope that people can recover, when they have such odds stacked against them. This illustrates how stuck individuals, families and communities can become when we do not understand addiction well enough, or when its treatment is undermined by social dynamics that isolate and exclude. It also shows how patient and dedicated staff have to be, to avoid becoming burned out by seeing the same frustrating cycles repeat time and time again. On the other hand, people did recover, sometimes against all the odds, and those stories of resilience never failed to provide inspiration and energy to continue the work. Recovery is contagious, and the inspiration and hope that spread through peer support and community networks are tangible.

This book mirrors my own learning curve, by exploring the stories we hear about addiction, and busting some of the more entrenched myths. Chapter 1 explores how the moral and medical models were influenced by the politics and social climate of their times, and briefly touches on some of the psychological and social models that offer complementary stories about how addiction develops. Chapter 2 moves on to look at the neuroscience behind addictive behaviours, investigating habit, choice and compulsion, and explaining how addiction develops from a particular type of learning. This is exploited by certain industries, including the computer game industry. Have you ever lost hours to a computer game when you really didn't mean to? We might choose to take drugs or drink alcohol, eat too much or play a computer game for three hours in the middle of the night, even though we know it is not the wisest course of action, and we will regret it in the morning. However, choosing to do something does not become addictive unless we are vulnerable for some reason, perhaps at a sensitive point in our development, and we repeat the behaviour until it has worn a compelling groove into the brain, and until we can no longer stop even though we want to. This is where the idea of 'addiction as a choice' becomes a little blurry. The more times we repeat a behaviour, the more automatic it becomes and the less of a conscious choice we make. Doing things automatically helps us run our complex lives, but in the case of addiction, habits that become automatic begin to trip us up.

Although there is a common process underlying different addictive behaviours, addictions to drugs and alcohol can bring with them extra challenges because of the way substance use over time can affect the brain's ability to manage functions like memory, planning and thinking flexibly, known as cognitive functions. Years of alcohol or drug use can lead to impairment of brain functioning. However, again, this is not just about the drugs (and alcohol), but also about the lifestyles that can sometimes go along with long-term use, particularly if you are not eating when you are using or drinking. Although alcohol and drugs do not 'cause' addiction, they are never risk-free, and it is useful to be informed about potential consequences. With better information, we are all able to make more reasoned decisions about what risks we wish to take.

There are many things that make us vulnerable to developing addictive behaviours, from our biology and genetic make-up, to our age, our environments and the lives we are born into. Chapter 3 picks up on some of these themes, looking at the way that addiction grows out of the interaction between a person and their environment, and the strategies that we develop to understand and cope with the cards we are dealt. If we face adversity when we are young or when we are growing up, addiction is more likely (although certainly not a foregone conclusion). Many people with the most severe drug and alcohol addictions have endured a catalogue of horror, including abuse, neglect and violence, to the point where sometimes maltreatment has become a normal way of life, and kindness is understood as merely the absence of harm. The medical model of addiction places the emphasis onto the symptoms of addiction, rather than the causes, which can blind us to the roots of some addictions. Often, addictive behaviours are not the primary problem but begin as a way of blocking out overwhelming distress, and then become a problem in themselves.

Chapters 4 and 5 begin to look at a psychological roadmap for understanding and treating addiction more compassionately, building on a global recovery movement. If sliding into addiction is an exercise in narrowing attention, gaining control over addictive behaviours has to involve a whole series of changes. We need to be able to recognise when we are being impulsive, or compulsive, acting without thinking. We need to think about the purpose of the addictive behaviour. What is it giving us? What need is it trying to meet? Understanding the answers to these questions can help us to find safer alternatives. We can then retrain our brains to form healthier habits, and to lay down new neural patterns to guide our behaviour. We might need to learn different ways of understanding our emotions and ourselves. We might also need to consider ways of building or repairing healthy relationships with those around us, to enable us to connect and feel secure.

Most people affected by addiction find their own way to healthier ways of living, or draw on the support of friends, family and their communities. If you are isolated or struggling to find supportive relationships, mutual aid and recovery communities around the world can offer a haven, and often a place to take the first steps away from addiction. For those who have been pulled into more entrenched addictions, often with other complicated physical and mental health difficulties, specialist services can be a helpful way of supporting the learning of new behaviours. Medical approaches to addiction have provided significant advances in reducing the harm associated with many different types of addiction, particularly some drug and alcohol addictions. However, it is when these are integrated with psychological and social approaches that we have a blueprint for making services more collaborative, and more focused on individual strength and choice.

Working in addiction services begins to feel inherently political after a while. You are working within a social and policy framework that often feels like it is working against you, even in a country with a National Health Service. What would an evidence based and more compassionate drug policy look like? Chapter 6 outlines how changes in drug policy around the world have led to profound progress in how addiction is treated, with many positive lessons to learn. There are now decades of evidence that drug prohibition does not work, and has led to human rights abuses worldwide. Waging war on drugs has increased problems relating to addiction, entrenched and strengthened drug-related crime, and left us with uncountable individual, social and economic costs: an epic fail, according to commentators ranging from Noam Chomsky to Jay-Z (Bandele, 2016). So what is the answer? There is an argument that decriminalisation or legalisation will just lead to ever more widespread drug use, and greater risks to our children. Why would we want that? Lessons from the way that other countries have begun to treat addiction may offer some solutions.

Recovery from addiction, despite the challenges and setbacks along the way, can be an intensely hopeful process. It is possible, and happens frequently, although you do not hear about it all that often because of that powerful disease story. A recovery movement that has been compared to a social justice movement (White, 1996) has led to the growth of inspiring communities of people in recovery, seeking to guide others trying to take steps out of addiction. In many ways, addiction is one possible result of what happens when our fundamental needs as humans are not met. The stigma around addiction excludes and isolates those who are affected, so creating a climate more encouraging of healing and support has to involve social connection and acceptance. We have some way to go in achieving that, but when we do reach out and support the most vulnerable in our society, we all benefit.

1

ADDICTION

From prejudice to compassion

Over the years, there have been many attempts to find a comprehensive definition of addiction. You might have heard it described as an unhealthy dependence on an object or experience, like drugs, or gambling, even a relationship. It's in our everyday language: when we say 'I'm addicted to chocolate', we mean that we want it too much, we maybe eat it too much, with the implication that we know we're doing something that isn't good for us. This isn't that dissimilar to formal definitions of addiction, with the defining feature being compulsive use of a substance (or pursuit of a behaviour) despite a wish to stop, and in the face of mounting negative consequences. It isn't about how much you do the thing – how much you drink, or smoke – but more about your relationship with the behaviour. In the case of drug addiction, manuals of psychiatric diagnosis reflect this in their criteria for a 'substance use disorder': you take more of the substance for longer than you intend to; you want to cut down or stop but can't; you end up spending lots of time in pursuit of the substance; you crave it; it stops you from meeting obligations at work or home or school; you carry on using even when it is causing you social or interpersonal problems; you become 'tolerant' (more on this below); or you experience withdrawal symptoms (APA, 2013).

These criteria were developed from historical studies of addiction, which included ideas around 'substance dependence', still a diagnosis within European guidelines (WHO, 1992). To be physically dependent on a substance means that your body is accustomed to it because you have used it over a period of time, so that you might need more of the substance to notice its effect, known as being 'tolerant' to it. If you stop using it, you might experience 'withdrawal' symptoms. Anyone who has ever experienced a hangover after drinking alcohol has experienced the physical withdrawal symptoms associated with alcohol. If you have ever been in hospital for a major operation or treatment, and been given opiates as pain relief, you may have experienced flu-like symptoms when you came home, as a result of the physical withdrawal symptoms from the opiate medication. In fact, if you have experienced these often-mild withdrawal symptoms after receiving strong pain relief, you may well have an inkling of what it is like to experience heroin withdrawal, as diamorphine hydrochloride, or medical-grade heroin, is commonly used in hospitals due to its success at relieving severe pain. It might not have seemed too bad, right? So why all the fuss about heroin being so addictive? Tolerance, withdrawal and dependence can be associated with particular drugs (and behaviours), but are not defining features of addiction, and are not even defining features of repeated use of every drug (cocaine and amphetamines don't cause physical dependence in the same way as heroin and alcohol, for example). Physical dependence is not the same as addiction. This might come as a relief to anyone reading this book who has just diagnosed themselves with a mild alcohol use disorder after a big night out, more alcohol than intended and a hangover the next day! Clearly, cultural expectations play a part here too. Harmful consequences of drug addiction depend to some extent on personal circumstances. If you can afford it, you might be able to maintain a high standard of living despite being addicted to heroin, and will be less likely to face some of the potential consequences around unstable housing or access to treatment.

It's also important to clarify that drug *use* is not the same as drug *addiction*, although drug and alcohol intoxication can lead to its own negative consequences. You don't need to be addicted to something for it to cause harm to you or other people. The whole spectrum linking drug use and drug addiction draws more social disapproval and stigma than other potentially addictive behaviours because of their criminality, but is drug addiction different to other addictive behaviours? The American Diagnostic and Statistical Manual of Mental Disorders (DSM-5; APA, 2013), the 'bible of diagnosis', has set out criteria to diagnose other addictive behaviours including alcohol addiction and gambling, with a question mark over video gaming addiction (more research required), but excludes compulsive eating, shopping, sex, workaholism and chocaholism. Although this may sound glib, you might notice that the criteria given at the end of the first paragraph to diagnose substance use disorders could potentially be adapted to many other behaviours. What about if you replace the 'drug' or 'using' with being head over heels in love with someone that your friends don't approve of? Do you crave your lover's company? Do you spend more time with them than you should, at the expense of other obligations? Do you waste time pursuing them or stalking them on social media? Does it cause problems with friendships because you know how your friends feel? Do you stop telling them about this new love and become secretive about what's really going on, even lying to people about it? Do you start to see their point eventually, feel angry with yourself and ashamed, break off the relationship but then end up going back more times than you meant to? Can a relationship be a 'chronic-relapsing condition'? The processes underlying any rewarding behaviour are the same, and all have the potential to become addictive. Addiction is a process rather than an end point, and can be understood as an extreme habit that has become dysfunctional, and is hard to break. The relapses, or failed attempts to reduce or stop the addictive behaviour, have been seen as its core essence: Professor of Psychology Nick Heather has defined addiction as "a repeated and continuing failure to refrain from or radically reduce a specified behaviour despite prior resolutions to do so" (Heather, 2017, p. 11).

DSM-5 criteria are based on a biological understanding of addiction and mental ill health, which understands addiction (and mental health difficulties) as brain diseases with biological causes. The National Institute on Drug Abuse in the US describes addiction as a 'chronic-relapsing brain disease', comparing it to other diseases such as diabetes and chronic heart disease. There are some difficulties with this view, which we will look at in detail later in this chapter. For now, it's important to point out that a biological understanding of addiction is necessary, but by no means sufficient, to give a comprehensive overview of such a complex problem with roots in our biology, psychology and social environments. Psychological and social models of understanding addiction place it in a developmental context, emphasising that it develops gradually over time, and can be more accurately understood as a learned adaptation to particular environments, but one that can become entrenched and compulsive. Different theories focus on different aspects of addiction, such as whether it is a choice (Heyman, 2013) and/or a way of medicating intolerable psychological or physical pain (Khantzian, 1985). In their extremely thorough review of 98 addiction theories and models, Professor Robert West and Dr Jamie Brown at University College London developed a 'synthetic theory of addiction', based on a multifaceted theory of motivation, which takes into account the biological, psychological and social elements of this complex problem (West and Brown, 2013). Their theory is broad enough to encompass the varying forms of addiction, and points out that addiction is related to other behaviours for which reason loses out to strong drives or motivations.

This illustrates a helpful way of seeing addiction. It isn't something you have or don't have, but exists on a spectrum with normal behaviour. We all have the capacity to become addicted to different things at different times in our life, depending on what happens to us and the opportunities available to us, and we all have the capacity to grow beyond it. It isn't that some of us have a disease and some of us don't. There are genetic influences to the way that addiction develops, but it cannot be reduced to a genetic vulnerability alone, even if this offers an attractive way of wrapping up a complex and messy problem. We can't fully understand addiction unless we are willing to put ourselves in the shoes of those it has affected, and to do that, we need to consider how effectively stigma compounds addiction in our society.

ADDICTION AND STIGMA

What do you see in your mind's eye when you think 'addict'? We are immersed in stories and images about addiction that stigmatise and dehumanise people who have become addicted, particularly to drugs and alcohol, and this can't help but influence the way we think about addiction and those who struggle with it. Tabloid media outlets paint addicts as deviants, weak and manipulative, or glamorous and tragic. The implications are that they choose to be addicted. They lie and steal to feed their irresistible habits. They're homeless, they prostitute themselves, they would sell their granny for a fix. They're *different from us*. These messages have created stereotypes of 'the addict' and 'the alcoholic' that are vivid in our social consciousness, and blind us to the myriad problems that feed addiction, and then entrench it in communities. They also blind us to the full range of what constitutes addiction. The use of illegal drugs brings with it the social disapproval of carrying out an activity that has been deemed criminal. However, there are grades of social disapproval, depending on your background and type of addiction, and the greatest stigma and moral outrage is reserved for groups that have already been deemed as 'other', whether due to their poverty or their different skin colour. One illustration of this comes from the numbers of arrests and jail sentences for young black men in the US and UK for drug-related crimes (Human Rights Watch, 2009). This group is over ten times more likely to be arrested and sentenced for drug-related crimes in the US, despite almost identical rates of drug use and drug dealing. In the UK, people from black and ethnic minority communities have lower rates of drug use than other groups, but are six times more likely to be stopped and searched for drugs, and are more likely to be charged with a drug-related offence rather than cautioned (Eastwood et al., 2013).

This stigma and prejudice continue to have far-reaching effects. Imagine that you've been drinking more and more, and you're starting to worry that you're getting a problem. Things start sliding out of control. Can you tell anyone? What will they think of you? What do you think of yourself at this point? What about if it's your drug use that's getting out of hand, but you don't identify with the stereotype of an 'addict' or a 'junkie'? All of your friends have been using drugs and it's been fine, so why is it not fine for you? Would you feel comfortable asking for help? What if you get locked up? What if you get a criminal record? The opposite is also true. What if you see how people treat drug users and drug addicts, but you've been using for ages and you're fine with that, as are all of your friends. People look down on you and judge you, so why not reclaim the 'junkie' label and turn it back on them? You've never felt so accepted as when you're with other 'junkies', so bring it on, they're your group and you'll stick with them. If people are treated as 'lying, thieving scum', some may try to live up to this expectation; others might internalise it and feel shamed by the prejudice.

The stigma surrounding substance use can blind us to the things that have led to it or keep an individual stuck, such as mental health problems, difficult or traumatic early experiences, poverty or social deprivation. This misattribution has serious consequences. Many people with the most severe addictions have histories characterised by traumas that most of us, thankfully, can only imagine, and there are high rates of mental health difficulties among those attending addiction services (more on this in Chapter 3). Stigma can reinforce the shame associated with both substance use and histories of trauma, which makes relapse much more likely. It influences how families and societies see addiction and drug use, and tends to breed pessimism about recovery. If shame and disconnection feed addiction, creating further divisions can only intensify the problem. Essentially, the stereotype of an addict is someone who is morally weak, who makes bad choices because they have a flawed character or personality, a view that dates back to the seventeenth century if not earlier, when loss of control over substance use and inebriation were seen as sins, and those afflicted as sinners.

You see the effect of these stereotypes every time addiction is described as 'self-inflicted', or in the catastrophic 'War on Drugs', announced by US President Richard Nixon in 1972, and adopted by most other countries worldwide as a result of heavy pressure from the US. This policy has entrenched addiction and violence in multiple communities around the world, and has led to people with addictions being dehumanised to such an extent that it is used in some countries to justify their torture and death (Kine, 2017). If addiction is a moral failing, then drugs are evil and addicts should be punished for their sins. Sounds pretty medieval, doesn't it? And yet we continue to prohibit substances in a way that bears no relation to the amount of harm the substances cause (Nutt et al., 2010), and we lock up young people and adults, particularly those from ethnic minority and lower socio-economic groups, because of their use of these substances. A vast gulf has opened between what we know about addiction from research and personal experiences, and the way that addiction is understood and treated in our society.

ADDICTION, DISCRIMINATION AND POLICY

The idea of addiction being a moral failing came out of the religiously driven temperance movements of the nineteenth and twentieth centuries. The 'demon drink' was thought to lead to poverty and crime, and destroyed families. However, from the earliest days of legislation designed to control consumption of substances, policies targeting addiction have focused on groups politically targeted as 'problematic' in society, and used in a discriminatory way. The Gin Acts of the early eighteenth century attempted to ban gin alone, due to it being "the principal cause of all the vice and debauchery committed among the inferior sort of people" (Dillon, 2002, p. 52), although other types of alcohol (those that didn't tend to be used by poor people) remained legal. Gin prohibition was repealed in 1743, following mass social disorder and violence, and the UK did not prohibit alcohol again, although there were a number of attempts. Temperance groups had more success in other countries, and alcohol prohibition spread across parts of the world including Scandinavia, Russia and the US in the early twentieth century.

At the end of the nineteenth century, Freud laid the foundations for psychodynamic theories of addiction, which interpret addiction as an unconscious defence against helplessness or powerlessness: a way to regulate repressed desires or unmet needs. These ideas have developed substantially since Freud himself, who theorised that addictions came into existence only as replacements and substitutes for "masturbation . . . the one major habit . . . the 'primal addiction' " (Freud's letter to Wilhelm Fleiss of December 22, 1897, from Masson, 1985). This isn't a theory that has been supported by empirical data. A number of years earlier, Freud had also written the first known description and study of the uses of cocaine, after studying its effects on himself, and recommending therapeutic uses of the drug as a stimulant, for digestive disorders, for asthma, as an aphrodisiac and as a local anaesthetic (Shaffer, 1984). He was in good company in the late nineteenth century. A number of drugs had not yet come under the class of 'sinful substances', and although opium use was causing concern, it was marketed in remedies such as 'Mrs Winslow's Soothing Syrup', to calm teething infants, up until 1930.

When drug prohibition arrived in the US in the early twentieth century, it actually had very little to do with drugs and more to do with racism and xenophobia. As with the Gin Acts in the eighteenth century, the laws that criminalised certain drugs over others focused specifically on those perceived as associated with particular groups. Opium smoking was banned in San Francisco in 1875, because of the association between opium dens and Chinese immigrants, while opium ingestion via remedies and 'tinctures' used by white, middle-class America remained legal (Musto, 1999). Cocaine and marijuana were targeted because of their use among African American and Hispanic populations, with the early advocates of drug prohibition openly illustrating the racism behind the discriminatory laws. Drug prohibition continues today, criminalising those who use even small quantities of illicit substances, without making a noticeable difference to drug use or drug dealing. In America, almost one in ten African

American men in their thirties is in prison, and the War on Drugs has been described as the largest single contributory factor to the racial disparities in the US criminal justice system (The Sentencing Project, 2013). The book *Chasing the Scream*, by the writer and journalist Johann Hari, offers a vivid account of the history and consequences of the War on Drugs. He describes the drug war as a search for

> easy answers to complex fears. . . . The public wanted to be told that these deep, complex problems – race, inequality, geopolitics – came down to a few powders and pills, and if these powders and pills could be wiped from the world, these problems would disappear.
>
> (Hari, 2015, p. 44)

In effect, drug prohibition encouraged the moral view of addiction to become mainstream, amplified the stigma faced by particular minority groups in society, and in doing so tainted attempts to understand and treat addiction with more compassion.

FROM MORALITY TO MEDICINE

Throughout the early twentieth century, medical professionals and others argued that addiction should be understood and treated as a disease, and were even jailed for their attempts to support addicts back into mainstream society (Hari, 2015). At that time, fighting to recognise addiction as an illness provided enormous relief for those stigmatised and excluded from society, and offered hope of treatment and care. In many places, it still does. This was a vital paradigm shift, and offered a more compassionate approach to helping people. Instead of being morally sick and wrong, people had a medical disease. It wasn't their fault. It lifted the stigma, to some extent, and mitigated personal guilt. It led to research into effective treatments, resulted in the production of medicines to reduce withdrawals, maintain stability and suppress cravings, and has reduced the harm associated with chaotic drug and alcohol use dramatically through 'harm reduction' approaches, described in Chapter 4. An understanding of 'addiction as a disease' grew alongside the 'addiction as moral weakness' idea for a time, with addiction initially being seen as a disease that affected those of weak morals, before this moved towards a 'biological vulnerability'. This was mirrored in the development of the Diagnostic and Statistical Manual of Mental Disorders (DSM), which has evolved its definitions of addiction from a sign of a disordered personality in 1952, to the spectrum of 'substance use disorders' described earlier in this chapter.

Today, the definition of addiction as a 'chronic, relapsing brain disease' is argued through research that has found that areas of the brain responsible for reward, judgement, learning, memory and self-control change during addiction, thought to be because of the toxicity of the substances. An extreme biological view sees addiction as biologically determined with a genetic basis – a 'ticking time bomb' for those with particular genes. There is no cure, but because it is defined as a disease, it requires specialist treatment from addiction teams and rehabilitation centres led by medical and psychiatric specialists, and demands that abstinence is the only option for long-term recovery. Research priorities are around isolating the faulty genes in order to develop medical treatments. However, as the neuroscientist and developmental psychologist Marc Lewis points out, *all* learning changes the brain, and addiction can be better understood as a dysfunctional and compulsive habit (Lewis, 2015). He and many others argue that the disease model has become a problem, and actually hinders recovery.

Why is the disease model so problematic? At first, it provided relief and compassion, and many people who have struggled with alcohol and drug addiction in particular see it as part of their identities. *I have a disease, I'm not bad, it's not my fault*. It still provides an explanation to families desperate to understand behaviour that can seem incomprehensible. At the most severe end of the addiction spectrum, the brain changes caused by decades of drug and alcohol abuse, alongside the equally (if not more) toxic decades of poor nutrition, poverty, poor mental health and self-neglect that often go along with it, can become irreversible. Recovery from this extreme position is longer and more difficult, and is more likely to require specialist support. Is this not the sign of a disease? While interminable debates over how to classify addiction can feel like ivory tower bickering and may be irrelevant to many people's personal experiences, it is worth considering why aspects of the disease model are damaging. The way that we define addiction influences its treatment. Understanding the flaws of the disease model will allow us to move towards a more empowering and evidence-based model, which doesn't reduce complex behaviour to our biology alone.

CHALLENGING THE DISEASE MODEL MONOPOLY

If addiction is a disease, it is unique in that some of its consequences are criminalised and its sufferers are punished in a way that would not be acceptable for any other physical disease. Diagnostic labels are useful in enabling communication and treatment planning. For example if the only way to access treatment is through receiving a medical diagnosis, you can see why it would be worth the label. However, seeing addiction as a disease may also increase stigma. Diagnoses of mental and emotional distress lead to assumptions that people experiencing such conditions are less predictable, less in control and less responsible for their actions (Buchman and Reiner, 2010). And what does it do to those that have the 'disease'? For some, as already discussed, it might be a relief, and an explanation for behaviours and situations that may have felt uncontrollable and overwhelming. It can provide a positive identity as an 'addict', or 'alcoholic', which provides a connection with others in similar groups, such as 12-step programmes like Alcoholics Anonymous (AA). For others, it may hang an unwanted label around their necks that is hard to shake, and reinforce the already existing 'us-them' dichotomy. Although methadone, for example, is an important part of drug treatment and can support stability and reduce harm, those that take it under supervision in a pharmacy sometimes describe feeling like "pariahs . . . second class citizens . . . it excludes you from society". The act of needing methadone, a prescribed medication, has become stigmatising in itself.

This model also skews our understanding of addiction towards the most severe end of the spectrum, which feeds pessimism about recovery. Out of the quarter of a billion people worldwide who used an illegal drug in 2013, around 10% will use problematically (UNODC, 2015), a figure that holds across different types of addictive behaviour. This is not to diminish the severity of addiction, but it is important to acknowledge that it is not the norm, even when exposed to behaviours or experiences that could be addictive. It might be surprising to know that recovery from addiction is the norm, and most people eventually stop or reduce addictive behaviours themselves, or through the support of their social networks and personal resources. Many are able to continue using their substance of choice, but in a more controlled and less harmful way. This is a challenge to the AA mantra, "once an alcoholic, always an alcoholic" (AAUK, 2017). The American National Epidemiologic Survey on Alcohol and Related Conditions (NESARC) surveyed 4,000 people who had a history of alcohol dependence and found that half had become abstinent or reduced their drinking substantially in the past year. Another quarter had improved a little, and out of everyone that had reduced their drinking, only a quarter had sought specialist help. The majority recovered, and did so without formal treatment (Dawson et al., 2005). This isn't just true for alcohol. The vast majority of people dependent on nicotine, cannabis and cocaine also stop using without treatment (Lopez-Quintero et al., 2011), and 'significant numbers' of people addicted to opiates recover naturally (Waldorf and Biernacki, 1981).

So what causes this natural recovery? In the sixties and seventies, there were suggestions that people who were treated for heroin addiction recovered at about the same rate as those who recovered without treatment. Those who recovered spontaneously (without treatment) tended to have higher self-esteem, better family relationships and higher levels of educational attainment – internal and external assets now described as 'recovery capital' (White and Cloud,

2008). Fast-forward to the present, and we now know that most people addicted to a variety of different substances just grow out of it, and stop using by the age of 30, although most have a few unsuccessful attempts to quit before they stop (Lopez-Quintero et al., 2011). If addiction is a chronic and relapsing disease, how is this possible? People who quit talk about life becoming more important than the addiction. It's as though there is a tug-of-war between the addictive behaviour and other hoped-for life goals like being a parent, being a partner or having a good job and keeping it. For those who are pulled further into addiction, a look at their histories shows some of the contributing factors. Their lives tend to be complicated by physical or mental health difficulties, they have fewer healthy social connections, they have had fewer years in education and they earn less. People in stable relationships stop using before their single friends, an unusual indicator of recovery from a disease. There are also more practical reasons, such as how accessible and available substances are and how acceptable they are among your peer group, which we will hear more about in Chapter 3. So although difficult, and with inevitable slips along the way, recovery from addiction is the norm, often without input from treatment services. Although severe addiction is often chronic, and there are likely to be multiple relapses before breaking the habit, this is one end of a spectrum, and not the whole story.

The disease model tends to encourage a 'them and us' approach. Doctors and health professionals see patients to deliver specific treatments for their diagnosed problems, and if they stick to their treatment and do what the professionals say, then they should get better. This is an ideal model for many physical illnesses, for which diagnoses lead to effective treatment decisions. It also works well with people who have severe addictions and need coordinated care to support their physical and mental health in order to reach stability. However, once stability has been attained, the medical model can struggle to help people move on from the 'disease' label, as psychological and social needs become more pressing. When we become physically unwell, we want to go to people with the expertise to tell us how to get better. And most of the time, we listen and act on the advice we are given. However, it isn't always helpful to see ourselves as passive recipients of treatment. In fact, if we want to change our behaviour, giving power to something outside ourselves makes any resulting change more fragile, not less. The strongest predictor of changing addictive behaviour is the belief that we can do it, known as our self-efficacy, in other words how effective we think we can be (Bandura, 1977). What happens to our self-efficacy if we label ourselves as 'diseased' or 'sick'? How does it affect us to think we are biologically predisposed to being addicted, or that we have an 'addictive personality'? What happens to us if we believe we are ill and must depend on a service to help us? These beliefs undermine the potential to build confidence in our ability to change and develop, and overcome addiction through other means. The more you see yourself as an active participant in your addiction, with choices to make about which way things are going to go, the more able you are to move away from those compulsions.

Diagnostic systems of understanding mental health difficulties and addiction (such as the DSM-5; APA, 2013; or ICD-10; WHO, 1992) provide a common language to understand what happens when our minds trip us up, and offer a framework for addressing these difficulties. However, it is difficult to draw the line between what is 'disordered' and what is not. When does a compulsive behaviour become a disorder? What about when a behaviour is abnormal? But is normal just what is socially acceptable? Our terminology for mental health problems and addiction is full of words like 'maladaptive' and 'dysfunctional'. However, from a psychological perspective, even unusual behaviours can be understood as highly functional. If you grow up in an environment where emotional expression is discouraged, it becomes functional and adaptive to suppress your emotions. When these emotional needs demand to be met (as they have a habit of doing), it is functional to seek ways of doing so that fit with the environmental rules that you have been taught, and the opportunities available to you. Maybe you get too drunk every weekend because you feel socially anxious without alcohol. You know this isn't good for you, but you're not sure how to break the cycle. Maybe you started taking drugs because all your friends did, and now you're using regularly. Behaviours that we repeat enough times become habits, and under certain circumstances these habits can tip into addiction. At what point does this become a disease? Addiction isn't something you have or don't have. It's something that develops in people vulnerable to it, particularly at sensitive points in their lives.

One last difficulty faced by the disease model of addiction is its explanation that addiction is driven in part by the toxicity of drugs and alcohol. Substances, particularly addictive drugs, 'hijack' the brain, so they must be banned. No substance use is without risk, but is it the substances that cause the addiction? What about other types of compulsive, self-destructive behaviours that some of us follow despite negative consequences? Do you work yourself into the ground because you feel compelled by duty, or because it's easier than facing your personal life? Do you over-eat because it gives you a brief moment of comfort and contentment? What about staying in an intense but destructive relationship that you keep going back to despite your better judgement? Eating, relationships, exercise, sex, the internet, dancing, even Harry Potter – a whole host of behavioural addictions have been described in the research literature. The same brain pathways that light up in response to heroin do the same thing in response to high-fat foods, giving us memorable headlines about cheese being as addictive as crack cocaine (Gutteridge, 2015). Advertising and corporations within the capitalist economic system actively encourage addiction to consumer goods of all kinds. The computer gaming industry researches and manipulates our addictive tendencies in order to keep us hooked to our screens. Addictive processes follow the same pathways, no matter the object of addiction, and although illicit drug use is criminalised, the slide from drug use to addiction has parallels with the development of other addictive behaviours. Canadian Professor of Psychology Bruce Alexander has reflected this in his definition of addiction: "overwhelming involvement with any pursuit whatsoever (including, but not limited to, drugs or alcohol) that is harmful to the addicted person, to society, or to both" (Alexander, 2008, p. 29).

Our understanding of addiction has been corrupted by the stigma and discrimination from which it developed, confusing morality and medicine. The disease model alone is not sufficient to understand or treat addiction effectively, and often exacerbates the problem through promoting passive and controlling treatment models instead of empowering, strength-based models, failing to promote recovery and pathologising emotional distress. It has brought compassion and a scientific approach to treating alcohol and drug addiction in particular, but in a social and political climate which criminalises drug addiction, the stigma is impossible to shift. The biomedical model and the treatments that it has developed need to be better integrated with psychological and social models in order to offer a comprehensive understanding of addiction, and effective, integrated interventions. There are many routes into addiction, and in order to understand it well, we need to consider how biology, psychology and our social environments interact, and to understand how each of us makes sense of our own experiences.

2

IS ADDICTION A CHOICE?

It is true that the brain changes as a result of addictive behaviours, but this is not necessarily a marker of disease. In his book *The Biology of Desire*, neuroscientist and psychology professor Marc Lewis points out that these brain changes are associated with all types of learning, and the brain is primed to change more rapidly in response to its most desirable and engaging experiences, whether positive or negative. It changes in response to every experience we have, starting before we are born. In the case of addiction, these changes lead to behaviours that seem incomprehensible. Why would someone decide to do something that is so obviously bad for them, and do it repeatedly? Why can't they just stop, or just say no? Do people choose to be addicted? These questions may be particularly difficult for family members and close friends of people with addictions, as they too face the trail of carnage left in the wake of addiction. As usual, the answers are complicated, but begin to make sense when you understand a little about how our brains work to guide and motivate us. The more we repeat patterns of behaviour, the more habitual they become, and eventually, the more automatic. It's more efficient, and frees up cognitive resources for other things. Addiction can be seen as an extreme form of this natural process, and this chapter will explain this process step by step.

UNDERSTANDING THE ARCHITECTURE OF OUR BRAINS

Our brains craft the pathways of everything that we have been and everything we do – all of our memory and experience is mapped onto its folds. A simple way of understanding the brain is to consider it in three layers. The deep subcortical brain, the oldest in evolutionary terms, is a bit like a lizard's brain, responsible for fighting, fleeing and, well, mating, as well as basic bodily functions like breathing and temperature control; overseeing our basic drives, instincts and needs. The next layer is more mammalian, a bit like a wolf brain. Wolves feel, communicate, play, learn and have strong social connections to their packs, because maternal and pack bonding are vital to survival. The limbic system is part of this brain 'layer', which is the seat of our emotions and memory, co-ordinating these functions with sensation and higher thought processes to assess our environments and work out responses. Sometimes when playing with young children you might wonder how far we have really evolved from being pack animals, with the rough and tumble play, quick aggression and as-quick return of love and affection. Finally, the most recently evolved part of our brain is the cortex. This is the part of our brain that makes us human, with the ability to reflect on our own experience, imagine multiple futures and set goals for ourselves, think up and solve complex problems. Together, many of these functions are known as 'executive functions', which is fitting as they act as the executive director of the brain, co-ordinating other functions into complex abilities and behaviours. These abilities have enabled us to adapt to every climate on earth, and some beyond, thanks to technological prowess, imagination and persistence in the face of endless challenges, as well as to concoct increasingly gruesome and inventive ways of destroying our environments and each other. We are nothing if not innovative "at one level, no more than meat; and, on another, no more than fiction" (Broks, 2003, p. 63).

Our brains haven't been designed in a neat and co-ordinated package, but rather have evolved over millennia to give us two key ways of processing information. One is slower, conscious and reflective, using the frontal parts of our brain (part of the cortex described earlier), directing attention like the beam from a torch, so that whatever the light is shining on is whatever we are paying attention to. Then there is the faster, 'quick and dirty' impulsive route, which looks after lots of unconscious processes, so some of the older, deeper brain parts in the lizard and wolf brains are involved, to do with emotion and motivation. Unconscious processes are always running, because these brain parts are involved in functions critical to survival. This means that they can sometimes distract and override conscious attention, and hijack slower responses so that we can find ourselves acting before we are entirely aware of it. As a result, our brain can feel 'glitchy', and at times we can feel like we are being pulled in multiple different directions as a result of competing goals, wants or needs. Think of the complicated feelings underlying all of the habits we think of as 'bad', when we want something that we know we shouldn't have. These glitches make us irrational, sometimes unpredictable and wonderfully complicated, all entirely normal parts of being human. And in these glitches lie some answers around how addiction can develop and take hold, particularly if we focus in on the brain systems that govern motivation, reward and learning.

HOW BEHAVIOURS BECOME HABITS

From before birth, our brains are growing and honing pathways and networks in response to our environments, and our interpretations of our environments. Our brains change throughout our lives, although there are bursts of development in early infancy, adolescence and into our early twenties. Our experiences shape our brains, and our brains shape our later experiences, in a lifelong feedback loop. What is happening in your brain when you are learning? When you have a new experience, neurons across your brain fire almost in conjunction with each other, recording the associations with this particular experience to help commit it to memory. This discovery was made by psychologist Donald Hebb in the 1940s, which is why this type of 'associative' learning is also known as Hebbian learning (Hebb, 1949). The more times we do something, the more efficient the connection between the involved neurons gets, and this is eventually embedded into the biological architecture of our brains. Our experiences change our biology.

The brain changes associated with learning are faster and stronger when they are driven by strong emotions, and this is particularly true at vulnerable points in our development, such as infancy, adolescence and our early twenties. As Marc Lewis describes, "the newer, more attractive, and more engaging something is, the more likely the brain is to change, and the more likely those changes are to condense into habits" (Lewis, 2015, pp. 32–33). A behaviour becomes meaningful to us in a strong and emotive way; we repeat it, and repeat it, and the more we repeat, the more habitual it becomes. This is true of thoughts as well as actions: the more we think in a particular way, the more likely it is that our thoughts will slide into that familiar pattern again in the future, particularly if it is emotionally meaningful. Say you go to a party when you are in your teens. You walk in, and you see a boy you really like. He comes over to talk to you, and you go red, and can't think of anything to say, stumbling through a conversation until he moves on. You feel a hot flush of embarrassment and think to yourself, 'I'm so stupid . . . why would he ever like me . . . he'll think I'm an idiot'. Neurons fire and connect. Later, when you are home, you replay the scene in your head, strengthening those connections, so that next time you see the boy, a pathway has been set up and you are primed to worry. If you have a similar experience, this pathway becomes even stronger, influencing your tendency to expect embarrassment in the company of this boy. If the encounter goes well, the pathway alters to reflect this, updating and broadening the network. In this brief example, you can see how learning spreads across many different parts of the brain: cortical areas involved in vision and sound, the limbic areas of the amygdala (emotion) and hippocampus (memory), the striatum (motivation and reward) and the prefrontal cortex (thinking and planning).

Behaviour is moulded through the interplay of rewards and punishments. If you're the person at the party, the punishment of the embarrassment could potentially shape the way you behave with that boy, with boys in general, at future parties, and in how you feel about yourself. If you've just learned to ride your bike, the reward of the joy of your achievement could pull your behaviour towards more bike riding or more confidence in your ability to learn. If you have ever studied psychology, you've probably come across the behavioural psychologist Burrhus Frederic Skinner, usually known as B. F. Skinner, whose experiments explored what he named 'operant conditioning'. Essentially, behaviour can be reinforced, or increased in frequency, if it leads to a reward (known as positive reinforcement) or the removal of something aversive (known as negative reinforcement). Skinner also discovered that if rewards are given intermittently or unpredictably, behaviour increases more, and persists for longer than if rewards are given at regular intervals. It turns out that humans behave very similarly to the pigeons and rodents who participated in Skinner's experiments. The more unpredictable a reward, the more likely we are to pursue a particular pattern of behaviour. Slot machines are designed to pay out small rewards fairly frequently, medium rewards occasionally, and the jackpot winnings very rarely. The small wins are programmed to happen randomly, but just often enough to make you want to keep playing: a design so successful that the bulk of casino revenue now comes from machine games, and for those who become addicted to playing them, addiction occurs three to four times faster than with other forms of gambling (Breen and Zimmerman, 2002).

The region of the brain most commonly associated with reward, motivation and addiction is the striatum, so named by the anatomist and 'founding father of clinical neuroscience', Thomas Willis, in 1664, because it's striped, or 'striated'. When we're deciding what to do, we need to consider the likely outcome of our action, choose which action to take, and shift our behaviour depending on the outcome of our action. Complex decisions involve lots of brain regions, but the connections converge in the striatum, which learns what we want, and decides whether or not it's worth going after. Part of the ventral striatum (the lower part of the striatum, so called because it would be on the belly side, or ventral side, of a four-legged animal) called the nucleus accumbens, is heavily connected with other brain regions: the frontal lobes which manage meaning and expectation, and also control impulses; the emotional alarm station of the amygdala; the insular cortex which translates internal states (like the experience of pain, or cravings) into conscious experiences; motor areas governing action; and cortical and subcortical memory circuits. The accumbens focuses attention, perception, meaning and action, and with enough motivation can send us after a strongly desired goal single-mindedly. How does this work in action? Imagine that you've been working for a few hours, you can feel your concentration starting to lapse, and suddenly you realise that you are starving, thanks to the insula's work to bring this state into consciousness, which it follows up with a rapid craving for sugar. The accumbens throws itself into action. You *want* food. It's a sharp impulse. Memories and thoughts of meals start crowding in from cortical areas, your frontal cortex starts wondering what you have in the fridge and planning recipes, the amygdala sends you a mild jolt – 'oh no!' – as you realise you forgot to go to the shops. The memory of the packet of biscuits in the cupboard flashes across your mind's eye. Projections from the accumbens to the orbitofrontal cortex (OFC: the lower part of your prefrontal cortex) trigger this part of your brain into a transactional weighing up of your options, assessing the relative values of emotion and expectation. 'I should eat something healthy, I'm watching my weight, but I've been working hard, I don't have time to stop for long . . . I'll just have a couple and then eat properly later.' The accumbens receives this information, and is narrowing your attention, and your craving is magnified, and it guides your thoughts into giving yourself permission, and a pattern of action is chosen. You fetch the biscuits and eat one while you go back to work, then look up five minutes later and half the packet is gone.

This whole process is fuelled by the frequently misunderstood neurotransmitter dopamine, which rushes up from an area in the midbrain called the ventral tegmental area, activating the accumbens and setting off a chain of 'wanting'. Researchers initially thought that dopamine was the 'pleasure chemical', because it seemed to be released in response to a reward, or something associated with a reward. However, it turns out that dopamine is also released in response to punishment, and also immediately before a reward is actually received, if it has been delivered in a predictable and repetitive way. More is released if rewards are given intermittently and unpredictably (Berridge and Kringelbach, 2008). What is going on in our brains here? Recent research has given us a more nuanced understanding of how this brain chemical works in collaboration with other systems and neurotransmitters to guide expectation. We are storytellers, and we love to find patterns in our lives to help us make sense of an often-unpredictable world. We spend time in 'mental time-travelling' and 'future-forecasting', and what we now know is that dopamine is released in response to *anticipation* of reward or punishment. It helps us to learn. The biggest spikes are found when an expectation has been met, or a pattern has been recognised, the joy of achievement and the knowledge that a goal has been reached. An example of this comes from some of the people with heroin addictions I worked with in Scotland, who talked about the urgency with which they would seek their drug, sometimes trudging through deep snow in rural areas to get to their dealer while 'rattling', or experiencing heroin withdrawal symptoms of sweats, shakes and agitation. Their symptoms would vanish almost immediately, not when the drug was in their veins or brains, but when the plastic baggy containing the drug was in their hands. Dopamine drives the chase and acquisition, the excitement and power, the 'I did it!', not the fulfilment of reward.

Remember Hebbian learning? As well as driving motivation and reward, dopamine also plays a key role in memory formation. Our memories of past experience guide our future behaviour, and it is dopamine release that learns which rewards are associated with which behaviours, and imprints this in our neural networks. Dopamine changes our brain wiring, through strengthening connections here, pruning others there. The more a behaviour is repeated, the stronger the networks become, and the more distributed, as dopamine gathers and associates more and more cues with the reward. In animal research, the more rats were shown cues which predicted their rewards, and cues predicting cues which predicted the rewards, the more these earlier cues triggered the nucleus accumbens, meaning that over time, attention was directed towards the reward from within ever-increasing circles, the dopamine flow started earlier and earlier and the craving and desire for the reward intensified. This was studied by the researchers Kent Berridge and Terry Robinson, who named this process 'incentive sensitisation' (2016). It's a little like a spinning vortex that gets wider and wider, pulling any associated cues into its flow and carrying them down to its focused core. Each time a new stimulus is included in the process of chasing the reward, it is tied into the dopamine web, a process which Berridge and Robinson called 'incentive salience', the dopamine flagging up this stimulus – 'This is important! Pay attention!' – so that a chain of cues is set up which grow further and further out from the reward itself, until any number of cues can set off the chain, but all lead to the same outcome. The more cues involved, the harder it may be to resist. Everything points towards the reward, so that the rest of life is poured through this biased filter.

Our brain is highly skilled at seeking out patterns. One of its glitches is to associate random occurrences, so we impose order on chaos. It makes us creative, but also prone to conspiracy and superstition. The association of random cues helps our brain imprint important and rewarding experiences so that we know how to find them again, and become biased towards cues that lead us to them. And anything can become a 'cue' or a 'salient incentive'. Many people who have been addicted to heroin talk about how silver foil can trigger dopamine-fuelled cravings and the flood of memory and desire that comes along with them, because it is used to hold and heat the drug before it is smoked, the roiling of the smoke across the foil giving it its name of 'chasing the dragon'. Internal experiences can also be cues, like anxiety, or the anticipation of terrible memories, so that a fleeting experience can set off a relentless chain of events. The more a particular behaviour is repeated, the more seemingly random cues might trigger the reward network, the resulting desire and the pursuit of the reward. This isn't part of a disease or a dysfunctional process in itself; it's just how we form habits.

Berridge and Robinson's research is important for many reasons, but a key message of their work is the recognition that addiction isn't about chasing hedonistic pleasure. Their work shows that the 'wanting' governed by dopamine is disconnected from 'liking' and that actually, addictive behaviours are a reflection of sensitised wanting, even when the reward is no longer liked. This chimes with the experience of people addicted to drugs, alcohol and anecdotally to food, gaming and other behaviours. At first, the reward might bring some pleasure, or relief from pain, but as the behaviour turns into a habit and becomes more compulsive, people feel compelled to chase it, even if they know that they don't want it, don't even like it, but they are being swept into the vortex and struggle to resist.

HOW HABITS BECOME COMPULSIONS

In most cases, these habits don't lead to addiction, but a couple of things make it more likely. The first is repetition, and the way that dopamine shapes the reward pathways to follow their urges with increasing efficiency, capturing more and more associated cues. As something is wanted, then acquired, wanted, acquired, the dopamine pathway gradually moves from the ventral, lower part of the striatum, to the dorsal part (the top part, like the dorsal fin of a dolphin), which governs more automatic responses. This part of the brain links cues with over-learned responses, making it possible for us to act without thinking and making it harder not to act when we want to stop. This is how behaviours start as conscious thoughts, but through repetition become more and more compulsive and hard to change. To many researchers and clinicians, this is when a behaviour, no matter how risky or damaging it has been before, crosses the invisible line into addiction (Everitt and Robbins, 2013). At this point, even if you don't want to act, and you're trying to stop yourself from acting, the compulsion is strong and the widening web of cues leads you into the beginning of the action before you're even really aware of it. This is the part of addiction that is sometimes difficult to understand, the sense that 'it just happened', 'I just found myself there', when it might feel like there were no obvious triggers or plans to act, because they weren't entirely conscious.

Generally, it is useful for us to have habits that are unconscious. It frees up processing power, and means that patterns of behaviour that are repeated frequently don't need to be consciously planned and acted out every time. A plan is cued in and unfolds automatically. You drive the same way every day to work, and one day take the same route, intending to turn off to go to a friend's house, but suddenly realise you are well on your way to work and have missed your turning. Your brain has picked up the cues that invoke the 'drive to work algorithm', such as leaving at the same time, being in the car and listening to your favourite radio station, and has sent you down your automatic routine because you weren't paying attention. This isn't abnormal or pathological. It's just absent-minded, a sign that our conscious mind has absented itself to other pastures, leaving our unconscious programming to follow its over-learned sequences. Continuing on a particular behavioural path in the face of negative consequences can be adaptive, and can help us survive. If some of us weren't compelled by love and duty to change nappies, soothe angry toddlers and endure sleepless nights, we might never decide to be parents. In fact, the same brain regions involved in motivation and reward are also those involved in bonding, relationships and love. Obsession, rumination, neglect of other parts of our lives and desire to continue on a particular path can indicate love as well as addiction.

The second factor is motivation, and the messages we are getting from our amygdala and orbitofrontal cortex (OFC). How much do we want this reward? How much do we need it? What is it giving us that we're not getting elsewhere? The first few times we chase a particular reward, the meaning of the experience is vital. Repetition and the regularity of anticipation intensify craving and narrow attention, but this happens more rapidly and with a greater impact when the reward meets something we need very deeply. Our emotions power the way that we learn by flagging up the things that are vital for our survival, and this is where the links between the striatum, the amygdala and the OFC, what Marc Lewis describes as the "motivational core of the brain" (2015, p. 81), really come into their own. The amygdala tells us how to feel about our experiences, thoughts and sensations, and what to do about it. It directs attention to the source of the emotion, amplified by the OFC, which adds some analysis and weighs up the relative rewards and risks, then sends the message on to other parts of the prefrontal cortex which add detailed reflection and deliberation. If the emotional stakes are high, thought becomes obsession, deliberation becomes rumination, and it becomes harder to draw attention away from the object of the reward.

Despite all of this, most people who use drugs, drink alcohol, eat fatty food or chase our bad habits do this without becoming addicted, even if in many situations we would rather eat less junk food, or spend less time on Facebook. What happens to the 'off-switch'? The part of the brain that inhibits the impulses of the motivational core is the dorso-lateral prefrontal cortex (dlPFC), but as impulse becomes compulsion, it can run into trouble. Brain imaging studies have shown that the dlPFC is more active in early stages of repetitive and motivated behaviour, but over time its control over the motivational core may falter, and in longer term addictions it can fragment (Goldstein and Volkow, 2011). Our conscious control mechanism is disconnected. This is why old habits are so difficult to break, because the more compulsive they are, the less open to conscious control they become. Rather than your brain being hijacked by drugs, it's as though your midbrain hijacks your dlPFC. It isn't entirely clear why this happens. One theory is that it is a part of the same process of Hebbian learning, as the reduction in use of these connections leads to pruning of the synapses involved, which shows up as 'reduced grey matter' in this area on brain scans. We know that this reduction in grey matter isn't because of damage caused by drug use, as the same reduction and brain changes are also seen in people who binge eat, and experience the same issues with compulsion and the depletion of self-control (Smith and Robbins, 2013). Most of the time, the dlPFC balances the motivational reward system, so that even when we are driven to repeat a well-learned behaviour, it will be able to put the brakes on. However, these systems develop imbalances for a number of reasons, explained in more detail in the next chapter.

Another theory is that conscious suppression depletes willpower, known as 'ego depletion' or 'ego fatigue', essentially that the more you try and push away urges and impulses, the more your willpower drains away, until giving in just feels inevitable (Baumeister et al., 1998). Attempts at conscious suppression just weaken self-control. Essentially, 'just say no' doesn't work, once the process of incentive sensitisation is harnessing your attention and directing your actions. The 'quick and dirty' impulsive processes capture attention and direct it towards rewarding cues, triggering behaviour while the slower, more reflective processes are still catching up. Once this process has been enacted, it is harder for conscious demands – 'Stop! . . . don't do it!' – to control the behaviour. Marc Lewis points out that shifting perspective and reframing your emotional state avoids this depletion of self-control: "Instead of tying yourself to the mast in order to resist the Sirens' song, you must recognise the Sirens as harbingers of death and reframe their songs as background noise" (2015, p. 185).

I suspect that most of us can think of a time when we have tried and tried not to do something, distracted ourselves, shut our eyes and have realised that the thing we're trying to avoid is all we can think of. This is just how our minds work: try as hard as you can not to think of a polar bear and the word itself conjures up the images, thoughts and associations you have with this animal. When the dlPFC disengages from our motivational core, we are left only with more childish techniques to suppress our impulses, so it can feel as though we are in a fight with ourselves – 'I want it I want it! No, you can't have it!' – until in many cases we are worn down and give in to ourselves. We might also notice that we are more likely to succumb when we are already tired, or stressed, or when other things are not as we would want them to be, so the relief, enjoyment or escape mean that much more. In brain terms, when we are vulnerable or off-guard, rewards might be more 'motivationally salient', and we will be more biased towards cues that suggest their availability. This was illustrated in the 1960s by the Stanford Marshmallow Test, designed by Walter Mischel and his team to study delayed gratification in children (Mischel et al., 1989). Pre-school aged children were told that they could have one marshmallow immediately, or if they waited a few minutes, then they could have two. Thousands of videos on YouTube portray the attempts of children to distract themselves by ignoring the marshmallow, touching it, smelling it, pretending to eat it, squishing, nibbling or licking it, and for younger children in particular, sometimes giving in to temptation. Things that we want, particularly those that are emotionally salient to us (and marshmallows are extremely emotionally salient to a three-year-old) capture our attention and jump up and down in front of us with immediate appeal, a mechanism known as 'delay discounting', or what Marc Lewis describes as 'now appeal'. This is another result of the dopamine surging through the striatum and OFC, marking the appearance of cues which signify reward as though there were a massive flashing arrow above them, and making future rewards or goals pale into insignificance, no matter how obvious or important they might be to us, or to those around us.

CAN COMPULSION BECOME DISEASE?

Whether or not you see addiction itself as a disease, it is clear that it can lead to a number of physical diseases. Food addiction is contributing to the obesity 'epidemics' described in the Western world, particularly the US. This leads to a range of health problems, including increased risk of heart problems and stroke, definitely consequences that fall within the 'disease' camp. Long-term substance use also increases the risk of many mental and physical health problems, as much a factor of the lifestyle that may accompany the substance use as of the substances themselves. Substance use makes it more likely that we will suffer a traumatic brain injury (TBI), which then makes it harder to control impulses and makes future risky behaviour more likely (Corrigan et al., 1995). Chronic use of most drugs along with the self-neglect that can accompany this can damage the frontal lobes of the brain, impairing judgement, impulse control, memory and emotional processing, so over time substances can directly impair the ability to control and change behaviour (Fernandez-Serrano et al., 2011).

The impact of alcohol on the liver is well known, with almost 1% of all global deaths being attributable to alcohol-related liver disease (Rehm et al., 2013), but less well known is the effect long-term and heavy alcohol use has on the brain. You will probably know about the way that alcohol can affect memory. If you or anyone you know has drunk too much, particularly on an empty stomach, you might have experienced memory blanks, and an 'oh no, what did I do?' kind of feeling, or might wake up and see regrettable texts on your phone that you don't remember sending. It should be no surprise to know that alcohol reduces our inhibitions and impairs our judgement. For some, this is exactly why they drink. Heavy use over time, though, can lead to more long-lasting effects on our 'cognitive abilities', or the abilities of our brain to manage our memory, language, perceptual abilities, and the 'executive' abilities of the frontal cortex like planning and problem solving. Some of this is a result of vitamin deficiencies, particularly of a vitamin called thiamine, or vitamin B1. This can have significant implications, including the development of a neurological syndrome known as Wernicke-Korsakoff Syndrome (WKS), a type of Alcohol-Related Brain Damage (ARBD). The impact of this syndrome can initially be subtle, leading to changes in our abilities to plan, or solve complicated or new problems. These 'executive functioning' problems are a bit like the executive director of a company just opting out for a while, leaving her sub-departments to get on with things without any overview. Although the usual routines will probably get completed, new tasks will be difficult to manage, and things might get more disorganised and less efficient, with different parts of the company pulling in different directions until it all collapses in a mess. The thing is, these are the abilities we need to notice a problem and change our behaviour to solve it, meaning that over time, heavy alcohol use and poor nutrition can stop you from being able to change your behaviour, or even to notice that you need to (Brion et al., 2014). WKS may not be so subtle at times, and the initial 'Wernicke's encephalopathy' stage, characterised by some or all of the symptoms such as involuntary eye movements or eye paralysis, problems with balance and gait, and cognitive difficulties, can be fatal if not treated with thiamine. If untreated, it can also lead to the secondary 'Korsakoff Syndrome', which is best known by a dense amnesia, or difficulty in forming new memories, as well as the 'executive functioning' problems described above. Our memory is what holds our life story. We use it to manage our daily habits, to know who we are and to function in society. Loss of memory ability can be devastating, and can lead to a requirement for long-term care.

Those diagnosed with problems relating to ARBD are often bewildered at what has happened to them because the impact of alcohol on the brain is not widely known, although the implications can be life-changing. When you ask people who have been diagnosed with ARBD-related problems what they want others to know, what they often say is to tell people that this is possible. Alcohol can rob you of your memory and identity, if drunk in heavy enough quantities, alongside enough neglect of your diet and other basic needs. The good news is that these problems are entirely preventable, by cutting out the alcohol to give your brain a chance to recover, and eating a thiamine-rich diet, as well as accessing available support. The earlier problems are picked up, the better the chances of recovery, and about 75% of people who develop difficulties will make at least some recovery (Kopelman et al., 2009).

SO IS ADDICTION A CHOICE?

As we have learned, habitual behaviours always begin with a choice. However, through the way that our brains learn, with enough repetition and emotional significance, actions become more automatic and less open to conscious control. You know there are alternatives, but they are hard to grasp. In the case of addictive behaviours, our brains trick us into sliding down a slope that is increasingly difficult to retreat from. As control decreases, can we still be said to be making a choice? Even in severe addiction, people don't chase their addiction all the time. This can lead to judgements being made about their intentions. If they can stop using sometimes, then they must be choosing to use at other times, right? As usual, the answers just aren't that simple. Professor Carl Hart and his colleagues demonstrated that people with long-standing addictions to crack cocaine will frequently choose money over pharmaceutical-grade crack when offered the choice in a residential setting (Hart, 2013a). This contrasts with the media storms about the drugs being so addictive they enslave people and make them crazed and out of control. Hart uses his findings to argue that choice is possible within certain parameters, but in deprived communities where there are few opportunities, drug use – even addicted use – is a rational alternative. Given what we know about incentive sensitisation, and behavioural reinforcement, it would be interesting to repeat Hart's experiments in more real-life settings, where those with addictions are more likely to be surrounded by cues directing them towards using. What would happen if the choice was being offered in the person's home, on the street or by a peer rather than a researcher? It's likely that the results would show that even within severe addiction, choice is possible, but the parameters may become narrower and narrower with the increase in compulsion and difficulties with self-control. As addictive behaviours continue, they may also bring with them mounting losses, shame and guilt, which can join the array of cues and triggers and tip the balance back towards the over-learned patterns of addictive behaviour.

No one starts out intending to become addicted, so with the benefit of hindsight you could argue that addiction is never a choice. We know that the slide into compulsion happens gradually, and there isn't a clear dividing line between a behaviour and an addiction. We also know that over time, the weighing up of costs and benefits of use becomes skewed in the direction of the addictive behaviour, choice is highly driven by motivation, and reason often doesn't get a look-in. It helps to think of control as on a continuum, with total control/super-willpower at one end, and total loss of control/compulsive automation at the other. We can be at different points on this continuum depending on many different things, including our emotional state, whether we have slept well, our history, social pressure, how we feel about ourselves, how many cues are tied into a particular habit, any number of different things, many of which we might not be completely conscious of. We may move up and down the continuum as these factors change, and we may be in different places on the same continuum for different behaviours. There are many things that influence our position on this continuum, within and outside us, which brings us to the next chapter.

3

IF IT'S THE DRUGS THAT ARE ADDICTIVE, WHY DOESN'T EVERYONE GET ADDICTED?

If you were brought up on the 'just say no' message of the 1980s, you probably soaked up beliefs around drugs being highly addictive and damaging for your brain. If you were exposed to hard drugs you could be hooked immediately. Remember the advert about your 'brain on drugs' sizzling like a fried egg? And the fault was placed squarely on the shoulders of these illegal and dangerous substances, which need to be banned to keep us from harm. This is understandable in many ways, as the deaths caused by drug use and addictions are clearly tragic, and illicit drug use is always dangerous. However, there are also some problems with this approach. If we understand that addictive behaviours follow similar processes no matter what the addiction, blaming drugs for drug addiction starts to get a little confusing. Is alcohol responsible for alcohol addiction? Food for binge eating and obesity? We have seen the consequences of alcohol prohibition, and we can't ban food, so how do we align this with the messages we hear about drugs like crack cocaine and heroin being so irresistible that if you have one hit you'll be hooked?

The theories about drugs being helplessly addictive came from studies on laboratory animals, who were found to self-administer drugs like morphine, heroin and cocaine incessantly under certain conditions, in some cases neglecting food and water until they died. Professor Bruce Alexander noticed that the rats in question were caged and isolated, and questioned the interpretation of these earlier studies. In 1977 he pulled together a team of researchers, and rather than housing the lab rats in the small and bleak cages of the earlier experiments, built 'colony housing', which included cedar shavings, other rats and lots of nooks and crannies for hiding, nesting and having some rat fun. They called it 'Rat Park'. These studies showed that rats living in rich and social environments took less, or no drugs even when they were freely available. It wasn't exposure to the drugs that led to compulsive consumption, but isolation and disconnection from a healthy and fulfilling social environment (Alexander et al., 1978). Later studies have shown that cocaine-addicted rats will choose same-sex snuggling over more cocaine, if they have the chance (Zernig et al., 2013). Humans, like rats, living fairly healthy and reasonably fulfilled lives also tend not to become addicted to drugs or other experiences. In fact, even with the substances that are generally seen as highly addictive, like heroin and crack cocaine, we know that just under 90% of people are able to use them without becoming addicted (UNODC, 2017).

Evidently, using drugs does not always lead to addiction, just as eating, having sex, putting a bet on and exercising do not always become compulsive. What makes it more likely that one person becomes addicted and another doesn't? Addiction is something that develops from a particular combination of ingredients, to do with vulnerable individuals having significant experiences at particularly sensitive points in development, within a specific context that maintains it. Individual vulnerabilities are found in the relationships between our temperaments, or our genetic potential, the emotional and cultural environments we are born into, and what we make of them. And there are qualities of certain experiences that are more likely to hook us in, but they are far from the whole story.

ARE YOU REALLY SAYING THAT DRUGS AREN'T ADDICTIVE?

It isn't so much that drugs aren't addictive, but that many things can be, given the right circumstances, such as being an isolated rat in a laboratory cage, with nothing around you except a bottle of water laced with morphine. Going back to learning theory for a moment, Skinner's discovery of intermittent reinforcement showed that the potential for developing compulsive behaviour increased when rewards were delivered in unpredictable and varying schedules. In addition to this, intermittent reinforcement also influences the *effect* of the reward. Remember when we first started to define addiction in the first chapter and looked at tolerance and sensitisation? Many people who use illicit substances take them irregularly, in varying doses, at varying times and in different places, simply as a result of the unpredictability of access and availability when you're using street drugs. This pattern of use works on us just as it did on Skinner's pigeons and rats, by sensitising the motivational brain network to be on high alert for any cues that the drug might be on its way, increasing cravings, and ramping up the 'wanting' of this dopamine system. This is also true of non-drug addictions. For those of us whose pattern of behaviour around a bad habit is one of restricting access, then giving in and bingeing in irregular and varying cycles, we are most likely making it harder for ourselves to find a more balanced pattern of behaviour in the long run. On the other hand, if drugs are used in smaller and predictable doses, tolerance builds up so that more of the drug is required to reach a similar effect, and if only taken to a regular schedule, craving begins to decrease. This is why opiate substitution treatments (OST) like methadone and buprenorphine work, because they offer a regimented and predictably scheduled dosage regimen that helps to calm the 'wanting' of the motivational core.

The other reason that OSTs work is because the substitution drugs have a longer half-life than heroin (so they leave the body more slowly). One of the things which increases sensitisation is a large 'spike' of reward, which wears off quickly, increasing the attraction of another spike, and another and another. Different routes of drug use are important here: the faster a drug gets to the brain, the more intense the spike, so injecting a drug places you at higher risk of your use becoming addictive, when compared to snorting a drug (as well as bringing with it greater risks to your health). With each repetition, the pathways in the reward and motivation centre are strengthened, and the cycle spirals rapidly, increasing wanting, while liking becomes disconnected. Marc Lewis calls this "deep learning" (2015, p. 172), to reflect the higher intensity and rapidity of the learning cycle. This is why rewards that offer a high intensity but short-lived spike are more addictive, in people who are vulnerable to their pull. Food addiction is more likely with foods high in carbohydrates, sugars, salt and fat, which are absorbed quickly and give a blood sugar 'spike' (Shulte et al., 2015). Stimulant drugs directly affect dopamine, so lead to more intense sensitisation of wanting and reduced liking. This is why substitution treatments don't work as effectively for stimulant addiction (there is some evidence for psychological interventions; NTA, 2010). Stimulant medication can work to treat attention deficit hyperactivity disorder (ADHD). In reducing the impulsivity associated with ADHD, timely treatment can prevent later difficulties with risky behaviours including substance use (Wilens et al., 2003).

This is also why some computer games are so addictive; the addictability of highly motivated repetition of behaviour is well understood by game designers. Many games and apps are designed to hook you in, feed you with intermittent and unexpected rewards, cheer you on with happy little cartoon characters and simple, colourful figures that capture your imagination, and lead you through simple and rapidly completed levels. These ensure that you repeat your actions hundreds of times an hour, until your dorsal striatum has your fingers reaching for the game every time you pick up your phone, even though your dorsolateral prefrontal cortex (dlPFC) is telling you that you need to put the phone down, delete the game and get on with writing the book that is increasing your stress levels!

So more rapid routes of use, combined with unpredictable patterns of use, increase the addictability of substances. In addition, different contexts of using actually change the experience of taking the drug, described by influential psychoanalyst and psychiatrist Norman Zinberg when he coined the phrase 'set and setting'. People learn how to experience a drug just as they learn how to interpret other experiences, by learning from those around them. 'Set' is the individual's expectations, intentions and personal features like personality and emotional state. 'Setting' is the environment, both physical and social, as well as any cultural expectations around the drug experience (Zinberg, 1984; Hartogsohn, 2017). The research in this area initially focused on the hallucinogenic drug LSD, finding that people who took the drug had vastly different experiences depending on their expectations and environment, and later expanded to include other substances. Cultural studies of alcohol use show that

> both mood and actions are affected far more by what people think they have drunk than what they have actually drunk . . . people who expect drinking to result in violence become aggressive; those who expect it to make them feel sexy become amorous; those who view it as disinhibiting are demonstrative. If behaviour reflects expectations, then a society gets the drunks it deserves.
>
> (Heath, 1998, p. 115)

The meaning we give an object or substance may influence its impact on us even more than the substance itself. Placebo drugs, those containing no active ingredients, have been found to improve a range of problems from pain to depression to Parkinson's disease. They are more effective when taken twice a day compared to once, when injected rather than taken as a pill, and change their effects depending on the size and colour of the pills taken (Hartogsohn, 2016). Even in situations where street drugs have been cut with so many adulterants that there is very little actual drug in the substance, people behave as though they are intoxicated and continue their lifestyle within their drug-using subcultures. This was described among heroin addicts in Vancouver during periods when the heroin on the street was so weak there could have been no physical effect, yet their behaviour barely changed (Hari, 2015). If our experience of drugs is so heavily influenced by expectation, are we more likely to become addicted to a substance because we think we might? Perhaps prohibition-led media campaigns are contributing to the problem. The context and pattern of accessing a particular experience or drug, and our beliefs and expectations, will all influence its effect. Some of these expectations and beliefs are set up when we are very young, and our early experiences can either heighten or mitigate any future risks of addiction, and whether we tip towards it or stay balanced.

SENSITIVE DEPENDENCE ON INITIAL CONDITIONS

Even before we are born, nature and nurture are intertwining in a complex dance to give us temperaments designed to help us meet the demands of the lives we will have. The scientific field of epigenetics has shown that the experiences of our parents are imprinted into their genetic code, and passed down from generation to generation. Environmental cues actually switch different genes on and off, determining how or whether they will be expressed. Our genes are best thought of as our potential, which is then sculpted into our weird and wonderful forms by the environment. Chaos theory in physics describes the way that an initial set of circumstances can evolve into wildly different outcomes within a complex system, where many varied factors dynamically influence, and are influenced by, those initial circumstances. This is known as a sensitive dependence on initial conditions, and the author and journalist Maia Szalavitz compared this eloquently to the way that addiction can develop (2016, p. 46). We are complex systems highly dependent on the initial cards we are dealt, even before birth.

Epigenetic research has shown how some of us may face an increased risk for addiction even before we are born. Our environments etch themselves into our cells, and the cellular enzymes surrounding our DNA, known as the 'epigenome', act as archivists that cut and paste, read and translate the expression of our genetic code into patterns that will be appropriate and responsive to the environments we will face after birth. Extreme experiences faced by parents are also encoded into sperm and egg cells, influencing their children's development even from conception. As you can imagine, the epigenome archivists are working overtime during foetal development, in order to try and prepare infants for the environments that their parents have faced. Emotional and physical hardship imprint themselves on subsequent generations through the genetic code, as well as through compromising how well parents are able to parent, despite their best intentions. This is our brain and DNA's way of ensuring that we are prepared for the environments we will meet. Women exposed to extreme stress when pregnant have babies whose stress response has been biologically influenced by their mothers' experiences. This is thought to be a result of greater exposure to the stress hormone cortisol while in the womb. For example, some children of Holocaust survivors have been found to have alterations to their epigenomes influencing the stress response, making some more vulnerable to stress and some more resilient, like a biological memory of the trauma their parents faced, and how able they were to cope (Kellerman, 2013).

Because of this complex interaction between our genes and environment, we cannot say 'addiction is genetic'. It is a multifaceted behaviour which develops over time and depends on the actions and interactions of multiple genes, which will each confer a little risk, or a little resilience. There are overlaps between the pattern of genes associated with addiction and other complex difficulties such as schizophrenia and bipolar disorder, as well as autism and ADHD, illustrating both the complexity of these difficulties and that genetic vulnerabilities can develop into different complex behaviours and personality traits depending on environmental triggers.

Despite this complexity in the relationship between genes, environment and behaviour, we love to look for simple answers to complex questions, and every now and then you see headlines announcing the discovery of the 'gene for binge drinking' or the 'genetic basis for laziness' (BBC Health, 2012; Gander, 2014). Headlines such as these are misleading, in that they confuse genetic traits with specific behaviours, dangerous in their encouragement of genetic determinism, in other words the idea that our genes inevitably dictate our behaviour, and can lead to hopelessness among people who are led to believe that they cannot change because 'it's in my genes'. As we saw in the last chapter, taking a purely biological view of addiction and mental illness can increase stigma, isolate people at their most vulnerable, and divert the emphasis (and funding) away from social, psychological and public health approaches better able to target the root causes and longer term consequences. As the philosopher Julian Baggini has pointed out, "too much attention to genes blinds us to the obvious truth that access to financial and educational resources remains the most important determinant of how we fare in life" (2015).

IS THERE SUCH A THING AS AN ADDICTIVE PERSONALITY?

The short answer is no, although this is still a feature of our everyday understanding of addiction. There are personality traits associated with addiction, but these have never been found to occur consistently in a single personality type. These traits tend to be the ones found at the extremes of the personality dimensions, and there are some gender differences in the traits that increase risk. For men, the outlying personality traits increasing the risk to addiction tend towards the adventurous, impulsive and thrill-seeking. For women, the risks are increased for those who might be more anxious, rigid and inhibited. There are obviously some overlaps in the gender differences, and some people might have both groups of traits. Having other mental health difficulties or neurodevelopmental disorders such as ADHD also increases the risk, particularly as a result of associated difficulties with impulse control, and the isolation and sense of 'difference' that sometimes comes alongside this disorder (Szalavitz, 2015).

How can such varying personality traits increase the risks of addiction? The common theme is one of self-regulation. Essentially, addiction is a failure of the checks and balances designed to help us manage our behaviours, relationships, emotions and appetites. As we saw from the last section, some of these personality traits may have their seeds in our genes and epigenome, but whether or not they are expressed depends on the interaction between a child and their environment. During infancy and adolescence, our brains undergo explosions of development. The balance between our temperaments and our early environment is the space that sets up the blueprints we will use to navigate much of our lives, and teaches us how to regulate our emotions and relationships. Lessons learned in these first few years of life can tilt our balance towards increased risk or increased resilience, and to understand this, we need to have a look at our earliest relationships.

HOW LOVE SHAPES US

John Bowlby, psychiatrist and psychoanalyst, is credited with recognising the importance of love, warmth and emotional connection for optimal development (Bowlby, 1969). He took an evolutionary perspective, recognising that young creatures without a strong attachment bond to their parents or carers would be less likely to survive. His theory of attachment suggested that babies are biologically programmed to attach to their mothers, and have instinctive or innate attachment behaviours designed to keep mum close by, such as crying, smiling and generally being cute. He also recognised that mothers (and fathers) are innately programmed to respond, creating a reciprocal dance of interpersonal connection. At the time of his research, a baby's primary need was thought to be food and safety, but Bowlby showed that our primary need is for love and responsiveness. He theorised that the relationship that we set up with our primary caregiver gives us a mental representation of relationships, called an internal working model, which becomes our blueprint for navigating our future relationships with others and ourselves. We unconsciously learn to do to ourselves what was done to us.

Our first relationship, usually with our mother, is most influential in the way we learn to manage stress and regulate our emotions. Our threat response is one of our oldest brain systems in evolutionary terms, involving the lizard and wolf brains we met in the last chapter, heavily connected to our 'newer' thinking and planning brain. The main characters are the amygdala, the almond-shaped alarm station, and the hypothalamus, a control centre that regulates unconscious functions like breathing, hunger, body temperature and our sleep/wake cycle. Also important are hypothalamic connections to the pituitary gland, which releases a number of hormones including cortisol, the stress hormone described in the last section. Think about what happens when you get a fright. You're crossing the road and a car suddenly appears, hurtling towards you. The 'quick and dirty' processing route from your senses goes straight to your amygdala. There's no time for reflection: this is about survival. It screams an alarm, sending messages via this system through your whole body. Your heart pounds, you tense and jerk back involuntarily. The car brakes and stops. The quick processing network calms down and gives way to the top-down thoughts of the prefrontal cortex, and you suddenly notice your heart rate, already slowing down. You're OK. You give the driver a dirty look, a number of choice comments on your lips, and you walk on.

Our threat systems are primed for rapid responses because in situations of real physical threat, acting fast is vital to survival. The threats that we face nowadays are less about our place in the food chain, but can be socially driven as in public failure or humiliation, isolation, social disapproval, being unable to feed your family, or feeling disconnected from your society. In addition, our brains are not always very good at distinguishing between an actual threat in front of us and a threat posed by our vivid imaginations, or memory. Imaginary fears can trigger the amygdala and send us into alarm stations. When the prefrontal cortex is short-circuited for that split second that the amygdala takes over, we have no sense of linear time. This is why we can feel as though we are re-living emotional memories when they capture our attention, and why soothing the over-wrought amygdala and bringing our reflective functions back on line gives us a way of processing emotional memories and managing reactive impulses. Our reflective processing allows us to return to the linear narrative of our lives.

It is our earliest relationships that teach us how to soothe ourselves. Our first threats come when we are very small, for example hunger, being alone or being uncomfortable. We're not very subtle when we're tiny; things are terrible or brilliant. A baby senses hunger, her stress system fires up and she lets out a wail. Her mother mirrors her stress, feeling a spike of dopamine through her motivation system, which drives her to act. She picks up her baby and cuddles her, making soothing sounds, works out that she's hungry and feeds her. The stress is relieved, and both baby's and mum's threat systems are soothed. A baby smiles and giggles, and his mother, and probably many other people who might be in the same room, make exaggerated faces, coo and smile. The baby is thrilled, and his dopamine pathways course through the nucleus accumbens, the amygdala tags the emotional and sensory aspects of the experience and marks them – 'this is important!' – ensuring that the behaviour will be repeated. These interactions also release a hormone called oxytocin, which over time strengthens the bond between mother and infant (and is also involved in bonding between friends, romantic partners and even with pets), making both feel contented and joyful in each other's company. Over time, the cycles of stress and soothing strengthen these connections, so baby grows up learning that loving social connection calms his or her fears.

These are the roots of our internal abilities to regulate our emotions. If we are upset and we are held and comforted, we internalise the ability to do this, and we become able to comfort ourselves or recognise when we need to seek support. We trust that others will be able to meet our needs, because that's what has happened most of the time. Our stress response system is wired to feel calmed by love, and to find reward from relationships. The pleasure and relief we learn from these early relationships are inherently motivating and governed by the same brain systems we met in the last chapter. This is where the relationship between addiction, motivation and stress relief becomes clearer. Our stress relief system develops through repeated cycles of exposure to manageable stress and responsive soothing. It's like building muscles in a gym. We need a little stress, or the muscles remain weak and don't get enough practice. If our every need is answered before we notice it, we have so little experience with feeling stressed that even molehills feel like mountains. In situations where there is too much stress, the systems become overwhelmed, and may either become hyperactive, as though we are responding to threats all of the time, or shut down and become numb and unresponsive.

These adaptations happen particularly quickly over the first two years of life, when we see a rapid expansion of neurons and their connections. As we get to know our environments, our brains learn what is most important for us. As we develop habits and patterns, we start to let go of connections and pathways that are less relevant or useful for survival, pruning and refining as we grow older. Even before they can speak, infants are learning the language of emotions and relationships. An infant facing an environment that is unpredictable or frightening will become highly skilled at scanning for threats, and will likely become more reactive and less reflective as a way of surviving. This is highly adaptive. For example, if you grow up in a threatening environment, pausing to reflect and deliberate may get you hurt, but being hypervigilant and reactive to threats will help you survive. It is not safe to stop and think if you live in a war zone. Your sense of time is altered, and focus narrows to concentrate on immediate needs. If threats are consistent and predictable, it is safer to be wary, to shut down your responses and become compliant, or in severe cases numb and shut off. If threats are unpredictable, you might become more impulsive and reactive, with the threat response on high alert all of the time (Crittenden and DiLalla, 1988). Infants in either of these situations may be ill-equipped for calmer and more stable environments, and may struggle to regulate their emotions effectively. They will also be more prone to later health problems, as a result of the impact that stress hormones have on multiple systems within the body. In the structured and predictable environments of school and work, they may struggle, as their abilities to pause, control impulses and concentrate won't have had much practice. Threats in early life make it difficult for young children to grow up into teenagers and adults able to regulate their emotions internally, making it much more likely that they will seek external ways of doing so.

THE IMPACT OF EARLY LIFE ADVERSITY

It follows that the more adversity we are exposed to in early life, the more likely we are to develop addictive behaviours, as well as other physical and mental health problems. This was illustrated by the Adverse Childhood Experiences (ACE) study, carried out by the American organisation Kaiser Permanente and the Centres for Disease Control and Prevention. The ACE study surveyed almost 18,000 people, asking them about adverse early life experiences, and analysing the connections between these and their mental and physical health almost 50 years later. The survey asked about experiences of physical, emotional or sexual abuse, neglect, living in a household with parents who had substance use problems, mental health difficulties, exposure to offending behaviour, domestic violence or parental separation. The results were groundbreaking. Poor mental and physical health were found to follow adversity in a dose-response way. People who had four or more Adverse Childhood Experiences (ACEs) were seven times more likely to develop alcoholism, over ten times more likely to have injected street drugs, twice as likely to smoke and 12 times more likely to have attempted suicide (Anda et al., 2006). In a UK version of the study, they were three times more likely to be morbidly obese (Bellis et al., 2014). A man who had experienced six adverse early life experiences as a child was 4,600% more likely to become an injecting drug user than a man who had experienced none (Felitti, 2004).

Adverse experiences were also much more common than had been previously recognised. About a quarter of the people surveyed were exposed to two adverse experiences, and one in six people had an ACE score of 4 or more. Take a moment to read through the list of adverse experiences again and consider what that means. One interpretation is that children experience more cruelty in their earliest years than we care to recognise. These experiences happen in secret, unspoken and unacknowledged for decades, masked by the addictions, mental and physical consequences that draw the focus of public and professional energy and attention and bury the original problems beneath layers of attempts to cope.

Not only does prolonged exposure to threat in early life alter the brain's stress response, it inhibits the growth of parts of the brain involved in memory and alters the response of parts of the brain involved in social attachment and regulation of mood. If the brain is in a constant 'fight or flight' mode, it cannot learn how to regulate itself and delay gratification (what's the point in waiting when everything could change in an instant?). Children whose brains are swimming in stress hormones can't focus, may struggle to trust and may become numbed to emotion, seeking stimulation and thrills, or they may become overwhelmed by it, seeking solace in whatever comes to hand. Discovering an experience that soothes despair, anger or hopelessness will be hugely rewarding and emotionally significant on an unconscious level. In the absence of safe touch and a loving relationship, drugs, alcohol and food all reduce amygdala firing, and may offer a solution once their soothing properties are discovered. As Maia Szalavitz wrote, "Drugs are powerful primarily when the rest of your life is broken" (2016, p. 133). If we have a deep and unmet emotional need and discover something that seems to meet it, that experience will be learned deeply and rapidly, and we are more likely to go back for more.

WHY TEENAGERS TAKE MORE RISKS

These experiences are most significant if they occur in our teenage years, when our identities are still developing. Most people who use drugs start in their late teens to early twenties, and as you might imagine, an earlier age of starting to use is linked to a higher risk of addiction, when substances and addictive behaviours may become integrated with someone's developing personality. Our 'self' is made of disparate parts which integrate during adolescence, so if addictive behaviours are developing, this can get in the way of feeling integrated and whole, and can make it harder to learn safer alternatives. About 90% of substance addictions begin in adolescence, although most people stop using or reduce use in their mid-twenties (CASA, 2011).

Most of us can look back on our teenage years and think of regrettable actions and unwise decisions. Teenagers can be easily bored, desperate to fit in, but keen to stand out. This is partly a result of our stage of brain development. The brain is being pruned and refined to fit its environment. We have a feisty impulsive system, driving us towards friends, potential partners and new experiences, but the immature dorsolateral prefrontal cortex (dlPFC) is unable to offer much emotional regulation or impulse control. It does not develop fully until our early adulthood, although the orbitofrontal cortex (OFC) and more primitive regulatory strategies from the limbic wolf brain have developed. This means that we have all the urges, but a less well-formed system for regulating them. As a result, young people tend to value immediate rewards more highly, can struggle to multitask under pressure, and are worse at delaying gratification: the 'now appeal' that Marc Lewis described, mentioned in the last chapter. People with addictive behaviours have a greater tendency towards 'now appeal' compared to the average, almost as though their brains are stuck at this developmental stage of adolescence, with its greater impulsivity and immature ability to inhibit those impulses. In some ways, a part of them is. The dlPFC is also responsible for our sense of linear time, and its immaturity during adolescence may also mean that it is harder for teenagers to plan ahead, as their brains are much more focused on NOW.

Adolescents are able to reason and weigh up risks, but because their cognitive control centres in the PFC are still maturing, their decisions are biased to the more impulsive and immediately rewarding, particularly in situations that are emotionally significant. And friendships and peers are particularly significant at this age; many teenagers are highly vulnerable to peer pressure. Thinking of the vulnerabilities outlined earlier, imagine that a teenager is enduring difficult experiences that leave him feeling despairing and trapped. Finding a way out, or a way of feeling better, is highly significant, particularly if it also involves cementing relationships within a group. The first time people use heroin, it's often out of curiosity, or because their friends are doing it and they want to fit in. Most are aware of the risks, but many don't recognise their friends in the sensationalist articles about addiction and 'junkies', and may have seen people using drugs without becoming immediately addicted. The further away from their own experience the media stories get, the less likely our young people are to believe them, which can leave them uninformed about the actual risks of drug use. The risks we take as teenagers also depend on the experiences that we have access to. In some deprived communities, where drug dealing has become part of the local economy, people cannot walk down their streets without being offered a variety of hard drugs numerous times, particularly if it is known that they have used before and might be a potential buyer. Experimentation might lead to more regular use, and the risk of developing addiction increases if initial use fills a gap in your life, no matter where this comes from. Becoming established in a group can also chip away at personal standards and values, and you can end up behaving in ways that you would not have predicted and may never have intended. Addictive behaviours are very efficient at filling a void. We are all searching for meaning and purpose, and the greater the intensity and reward of those initial experiences, the more meaningful they are to us, particularly if we are vulnerable. This is where the development of addiction begins to diverge from more controlled or regulated use.

THE SEARCH FOR MEANING

When you ask people who have been addicted to heroin what that first use meant to them, they use the language of love and nurturing. 'It felt like a warm, soft blanket', 'It was like I had a family', 'It just made everything go away'. People are presented with a feeling they may not even have realised they were missing, and suddenly have a way of feeding a deeply unconscious emotional hunger. This experience will be marked as highly significant, priming the motivation system to want more. Overwhelmed stress systems will wire to experiences that soothe them, especially when nothing else has. However, the heroin, or whatever the drug or experience is that they have found, will not soothe the void for long, leaving an even greater yearning to feel safe, loved or just normal. As described in the introduction, this is the 'hungry ghost mode' of Tibetan Buddhism: "So long as we stay in the hungry ghost mode, we'll never know [what we need]. We haunt our lives without being fully present" (Maté, 2010, p. 1). If we are not provided with the opportunities to learn to regulate our emotions within safe and nurturing relationships when we grow up, we don't learn how to cope with distress or suffering in healthy ways, although we can develop the abilities in later life with the right care and attention.

Many of those stuck in the 'hungry ghost' mode, with the most severe addictions, have experienced brutally traumatic experiences as children, or a long and relentless 'drip-feed' of isolation, bullying or neglect. These are men and women who became violent after making a childish promise to never allow anyone to hurt them again, or who were told that they should have been aborted, or who were screamed at, beaten, witnessed repeated violence, were starved of affection and nurturing or experienced sexual abuse from sometimes multiple perpetrators, most of whom were not brought to justice. They may have done things themselves that they are deeply ashamed of. They were not protected, and were failed by social safety nets. These types of experiences aren't unusual within those attending specialist addiction services. Using the statistics from the ACE study, author Johann Hari points out that child abuse is as likely to cause drug addiction as obesity is to cause heart disease (2015, p. 160). One study of people attending substance misuse services found that 100% had been exposed to traumatic situations, with figures showing that 25%–50% experience symptoms of post-traumatic stress disorder (PTSD: Gielen et al., 2012). Between 75% and 85% also have other mental health diagnoses, such as anxiety, depression and personality disorder (Weaver et al., 2003), which also have roots in early life adversity. When you explore the development of addictive behaviours and mental health difficulties, it becomes easier to understand that they arise from attempts to adapt to prolonged and sometimes relentless confusion, distress or trauma.

However, not every child with a traumatic history grows up to develop addictive behaviours or mental health difficulties. Exposure to adversity, poverty, violence and trauma increase the risks, but there are many people who experience these events and go on to lead healthy and successful lives. Risk and vulnerability are not set in stone, but are shifting and responsive to our experience. Many factors can mitigate the effects of adverse experiences, but the most protective is a strong and loving relationship. If children have even one safe, nurturing and secure adult in their lives, they may overcome multiple adversities because they know that if they fall, there will be a safety net to catch them. It's important to note that parents are more able to provide these relationships when they are also supported and secure. Education can increase access to safe and caring adults, and allow the development of hope through literature, music and art, which demonstrate that other lives and ways of expressing yourself are possible. This is also why connection and caring relationships as adults are so vital to recovery. It also explains why some adults who have experienced other people as consistently abusive may find solace and the most enduring attachments with their pets. The social environment is also important, dictating access and availability to addictive experiences, as well as influencing the expectations and social norms of families and communities.

All of this shows us that addiction is about need, and the timing and pattern of exposure to certain experiences. It is complicated, and it isn't that helpful to see it as just about the drugs, or just about our genes. No matter where we come from, we have the same fundamental needs. The psychologist Abraham Maslow created a 'hierarchy of needs' that outlined our basic requirements for food and water, through safety and health, moving up to social and emotional needs, right up to our more 'spiritual' needs for meaning and purpose

(Maslow, 1943). In times of threat, we are focused on survival and the lower rungs of this hierarchy. In our current times, in this 'age of austerity', whole communities have been forced into this position, without ready access to food, heating and secure housing. Until these needs are met, it is difficult to look beyond to meet social, relationship and emotional needs. That doesn't make them any less valid, and if we are denied the hope of a meaningful life and a viable future for ourselves and our families, the 'risk factors' mount up, and addiction and mental health difficulties increase. To find balance, we need to address not just individual difficulties, but the social and political climate which can either limit opportunities and increase risk, or promote hope and environments in which we can meet our full potential.

4

YOU CAN TEACH AN OLD DOG NEW TRICKS

Addiction and recovery

If we can learn our way into addiction, can we learn our way out again? If the brain changes as addiction develops, forming those neural pathways that deepen with repetition and are difficult to climb out of, then can we develop new behaviours? Form new pathways? In order to work out how to do this, we need to understand recovery. This chapter and the next will look at how we can encourage recovery from addictive behaviours, from both individual and group perspectives. Is it all just about growth and learning? The psychologist Scott Kellogg suggests that rather than recovery, we are talking about liberation. Addiction traps and enslaves us, narrowing and focusing our minds and lives, so expanding and opening up again is about empowerment and freedom (Kellogg, 2016).

HOPE AND RECOVERY

A revolution has been taking place in the way that mental illness and addiction are understood, driven by those who have rejected the labels and stigma arising from moral and medical models of psychological distress and addictive behaviour. Psychiatric diagnoses are useful in providing a common language for understanding confusing symptoms, and providing access to benefits and services. However, they reduce the complexity of human experience and distress to simple categories, and lull us into a false sense of security, suggesting that complexity can be treated with simple algorithms. With each iteration of the diagnostic manuals, more and more examples of distress are gathered into the net of 'mental illness'. However, we are yet to find a 'biological basis for schizophrenia', just as we are yet to find a 'biological basis for addiction', beyond the variable influence of multiple genes. 'Survivor' and user groups have defined a new approach to recovery, which incorporates the need to find hope for the future, to develop resilience, to find a sense of connection to others and your community, and as a result, to forge a stronger and more empowered identity. They question how much the loss of these things is driven by the medicalisation of their difficulties, and the encouragement to be passive recipients of treatment, as outlined in Chapter 1. Recovery from addictive behaviours means different things to different people, so the UK Drug Policy Commission Recovery Consensus Group developed the following definition: "the process of recovery from problematic substance use is characterised by voluntary sustained control over substance use which maximises health, wellbeing and participation in the rights, roles and responsibilities of society" (UKDPC, 2008). Although this is specific to substance use, it could apply just as well for other addictive behaviours. Recovery isn't just about changing the addictive behaviour; it's about learning how to live differently. Just as we learn helplessness, we can learn optimism (Seligman, 2002), and the hope surrounding people in recovery is contagious.

BUT ADDICTS ARE ALL IN DENIAL! HOW CAN YOU HELP SOMEONE IF THEY DON'T WANT HELP?

There is a story that paints people with addictions as 'resistant to change', or 'in denial'; their heads in the sand about problems that seem huge and apparent to the people around them. To the friends and family of the person with addiction, denial might seem obvious. 'He just can't see it. . . . she's ignoring the debt. . . . he's not opening his letters any more . . . she just won't listen'. This has been seen as inherent to the addiction, when actually it is part of someone defending themselves against a perceived attack on the very essence of who they are, or want to be. Perhaps a better way of understanding it is in terms of a 'cognitive bias', or the way we selectively attend to information that confirms our existing beliefs. If there are things that seem inconsistent with truths that any of us hold dear, or if those truths challenge us in ways that we might not be ready to accept, we basically just ignore them. We all do this to some extent. Denial and resistance aren't static states, or to do with a particular individual, but are processes that emerge from the interpersonal dynamics in a relationship. The more directly challenged someone feels, the more likely they will resist the challenge. The more they feel that someone is standing alongside them without judging, the more likely they are to express their own doubts and concerns about the situation. It's both about how the message is relayed, and how ready the person is to hear it. Does it matter if we call it denial or a cognitive bias? It does, only because of the extra negativity given to the term 'denial' in addiction, and the lack of recognition that this is an aspect of our normal defence against distress and inconsistencies in our personal stories. It is also important because beliefs about denial in addiction have led to punitive interventions seeking to 'break through' the denial and confront people with the consequences of their behaviour. It is true that priorities shift during addiction, and people often act in ways that they later regret, but it is notable that the deception and lying associated with addiction often disappear when someone knows they will not face punishment or judgement. The deception may be more a product of the punishment than the addiction. However, as Maia Szalavitz has pointed out, punishing people for a problem defined by its resistance to punishment is a task doomed to failure (2016).

Think of it like this. You're feeling out of control and ashamed because you know that your relationship with food/alcohol/cocaine is unhealthy. But you also know that if you didn't binge/use you would have to face the anxiety/trauma/feelings of inadequacy which also made you feel ashamed and isolated. In this instance, someone telling you that your behaviour is wrong is likely to increase your shame, and therefore inadvertently reinforce the problem. You are more likely to resist them, ignore them or even attack them, if it feels like they are threatening something very private and personal to you. It is difficult to accept the reality of a situation we don't like, particularly if we feel ashamed and guilty about it, if there are underlying needs that we haven't admitted or accepted, and if we are afraid of giving up something that feels like a lifeline even if we know it's bad for us. However, all of these fears can be overcome in the context of a supportive and non-judgemental relationship which offers hope and acceptance. We need to assume that people have very good reasons for persisting in behaviours that, to us, seem harmful and destructive, and we just need to find them. How would they feel if they gave up the behaviour? What if, to them, that prospect is worse than continuing? Accepting this assumption is easier said than done, especially if you are the family member or friend of someone with an addiction that may have directly impacted you. There are particular approaches that can be useful for families set out in the next chapter.

For many people the first steps towards change include connecting with someone or something that instils hope, allowing you to believe that maybe things can change. Sometimes the need to change comes from some external force, such as a criminal charge in the case of drug use, or pressure from others. As discussed in the last chapters, most people with addictions recover without professional support, drawing on the social support and resources around them to develop control and change their behaviour. Those who are able to use their own resilience and networks to alter an addictive behaviour tend to have better social support, better education, have experienced less adversity and sometimes have more financial resources at their disposal. For those who do seek help, there are many options available. Addiction is complex, and medical, psychological and social approaches may be more or less helpful at different stages, because as we now know, there are biological, psychological and social aspects to the ways that addictive behaviours develop and progress.

WHY RELATIONSHIPS ARE THE KEY TO RECOVERY

Treatment for addiction is at its most effective when it is delivered within a framework of compassion and understanding. Offering respect, empathy and a collaborative, non-judgemental approach is the basis of all therapeutic relationships (Rogers, 1961). People with histories involving traumas from bullying and isolation right the way through to severe and repeated interpersonal abuse are not going to trust very easily, and are highly sensitive to any sign of criticism or rejection. They are also skilled at assessing your emotions and motivations as a result of their skills in analysing unpredictable environments, and are likely to pick up on any hints of inauthenticity, boredom or 'winging it'. Effective treatment is about considering individuals' behaviour in light of 'what has happened to them' and 'how is that affecting them now' rather than 'what is wrong with them'. The power of these relationships cannot be underestimated, and may be someone's first experience of genuine warmth and care.

This ethos does not mean accepting every aspect of behaviour without challenge. It is just that a therapeutic relationship provides a strong-enough connection within which to challenge empathically, and support someone to place limits on the parts of themselves they are seeking to change. These relationships provide the sensitive and responsive social scaffolding that hold the pieces of someone's imagined future in place while they reach towards them. Sometimes, a useful conversation is all it takes to tip the balance for someone to begin to make changes.

REDUCING HARM: MEDICAL APPROACHES TO TREATMENT

A compromise position on the 'addiction as disease' versus 'addiction as entrenched learning' dichotomy is the comparison of severe addiction to a chronic health condition like diabetes or heart disease. This is a way of making the medical and psychosocial models fit more closely, and recommends suitable treatment in the form of 'self-management', which aims to manage wellbeing and sustain recovery. Although some of the difficulties of seeing addiction as a disease still stick, this can be a helpful way of thinking about recovery for those who prefer to see their difficulties as a manifestation of illness. Learning how to manage a disease is about addressing any obstacles that get in the way of change. For diabetes, this might be about diet and exercise. For addiction, it could be education, employment, housing, rebuilding relationships or addressing other mental health difficulties. It offers a broad church: recovery under this approach could mean abstinence, but also harm minimisation, controlled use or stabilisation.

There is a long-standing and passionate debate over the merits of abstinence versus a 'harm reduction' approach in the field of treatment for problematic drug use and addiction. Harm reduction advocates accept that some people will continue to use drugs, and so should be supported to use more safely, often with a goal of gradually reducing and stopping use. Abstinence advocates see harm reduction as 'enabling' drug use, and believe that abstinence is the only option for 'true' recovery. Abstinence-specific social support is important in promoting recovery from *severe* drug or alcohol addiction (Litt et al., 2007), but both options are important in an integrated view of recovery, and the best goal (and the one most likely to work) is the one chosen by the individual. There are three broad goals of harm reduction: 'staying alive', which includes interventions around overdose prevention and safe injecting; 'maintaining health', such as providing treatment for blood-borne viruses, needle exchanges, opiate substitution treatments (described below), drug testing in festivals and clubs and safe injecting rooms; and 'getting better', which is where the psychological and social interventions come in, integrated with pharmacological approaches where necessary (Wodak, 1994; Kellogg, 2003). All start with the need to meet the person 'where they're at'. Clinical psychologist and author Andrew Tatarsky has integrated harm reduction with psychotherapy (2003), and emphasises that the middle ground of this debate may be 'abstinence eventually', as any gradual steps towards this possible goal are steps in the right direction. This has been defined as 'gradualism' by clinical psychologist and author Scott Kellogg (2003).

Opiate substitution prescriptions such as methadone and buprenorphine (Suboxone or Subutex) provide a vital way to stabilise a chaotic lifestyle focused on chasing the next fix, and also try to shift sensitisation to tolerance by prescribing the substitute drug in a scheduled and regular dosage. They are slow-onset and long-acting, so reduce the highs and crashes of heroin (Clinical Guidelines, 2017). A drug called naloxone blocks opiate receptors, and when administered reverses the effects of heroin, and can therefore reverse opiate overdose. National campaigns have ensured access and availability of this life-saving drug for people using heroin, so that those likely to be first on the scene at an overdose have a way of preventing it. Medicines have also been developed to address other symptoms associated with addictive behaviours, such as cravings and withdrawal symptoms, although a review of these is beyond the scope of this book.

Where the medical model struggles is in the 'what next?' Pharmacological treatments in conjunction with harm reduction interventions are highly effective at stabilising chaos and providing a pathway for people to access care and support. However, as the chaos subsides, individuals sometimes experience a deterioration in their mental health, as the reality of their lives and history catches up. One of the criticisms of opiate substitution treatments (OST) is that they 'park' people, and swap them into a different form of drug dependence. They can be inconvenient, making people travel to clinics or pharmacies to pick up their dose, where they may be required to take it in front of a pharmacist. This can feel stigmatising. However, for many, this is better than the alternative of street addiction, and they are undoubtedly life-saving medications. OSTs are a way of providing stability, to give you a chance to look at the other parts of your life that need some work, but they can't help with everything. This is where psychological and social approaches, integrated with medications that can maintain the stability, come into their own.

PSYCHOLOGICAL APPROACHES TO TREATMENT

Rather than seeking to diagnose, psychological interventions are based on a formulation of someone's difficulties. This is an explanation of how the difficulties have developed and what maintains them, integrating information from the body, emotions, thoughts and social aspects of a person's experience. It combines the therapist's knowledge of psychological theory and evidence with a person or family's own thoughts and understanding of what is going on, and how the situation has developed. It's a bit like jointly doing a jigsaw puzzle, to show the overall picture of what is going on. Discussing and agreeing on a formulation can be an intervention in itself, as it is a chance for the individual to feel understood and an opportunity to see how some difficulties might relate to each other. It provides a map for how best to proceed.

There are many psychological interventions, including behavioural and cognitive behavioural approaches, which look at how our interpretations of events influence our actions. There are also therapies that have integrated Buddhist practices of acceptance, compassion and mindfulness, and many strategies for learning skills to regulate emotions and manage impulses. These are more or less useful at different points along the spectrum of addiction severity. The more severe and compulsive the addiction, the more automatic the behaviour, so interventions like cognitive therapy, which asks you to think and reflect, will be difficult. At this stage, practical interventions focusing on behaviour and environment are more helpful, because they provide concrete instructions for what to do in different situations. For instance, if your alcohol binges are triggered by receiving your Friday pay cheque, set up direct debits to make sure your bills go out, give your bank card to a (very trusted) friend or family member, or make a plan to do something incongruent with meeting friends in the pub, such as going to the gym. If X then Y. These are useful interventions in the short term, and provide a chance to find some structure, impose a little order on the chaos.

However, they are not sufficient: many people talk about the intolerable boredom and isolation that awaits them when they have cut off contact with drinking or using friends, and have stopped frequenting locations where they know they will be tempted. If the object of addiction has been filling a void, cutting off contact with it might be healthier, but leaves you exposed to the void itself. At this point, cravings might increase, and there might be a dip in mood; 'I thought I'd feel better when I stopped but I feel worse! This is worse than before! What's the point in stopping at all?' This brings us to the ambivalence at the heart of the addiction, and exploring this carefully is a way to make sure that our motivation doesn't falter in pursuit of the goals that we truly want, rather than the ones that we are being directed towards by our overactive incentive/reward system.

The conflict in the midst of addiction

When addicted to something, multiple associations, memories and compulsion will push behaviour down this well-worn groove. The motivation to change behaviour can come from many directions, from an internal recognition that you can no longer continue on this path, or from the external pressure from friends and family, or mandatory pressure from the criminal justice system. This can be distilled down into a conflict between current behaviour and core values, how you see yourself, or who you want to be. For some, it may be the realisation that you have crossed the invisible line into addiction. You feel like you can't stop, but now you really want to. For others, it is the recognition that they will lose their children if they don't stop, or their jobs, or their lives. The motivation to change is fed by hope that change is possible, which runs through the stories from mutual aid and recovery communities, and the inspiration provided by meeting those who have been through addiction and have come out the other side. It is also fed by the belief that you can change, even if initially that may come from others, because you can't yet see the light at the end of the tunnel. The tipping of the balance towards change is sometimes a revelation, and sometimes subtle, and often the scales tip too frequently back towards the addiction, whether this is through associates, environment, availability of the object of addiction, fear of facing reality, or just the power of compulsion. So how do we encourage people to change, and continue changing? How do any of us change?

Motivation used to be thought of as a static state: you are motivated or you're not. However, it is now recognised as a dynamic and sometimes fickle thing, which might vary depending on where we are and who we are speaking to. When any of us are considering making a big life change, it is rare that we are 100% certain about what we are going to do, and in order to explore our ambivalence it is helpful to give a voice to both sides of the story. Motivational Interviewing (MI) is a style of conversation based on self-perception theory (which says that we are more likely to do the things that we hear ourselves say out loud; Bem, 1972). It uses counselling skills, so is collaborative, empathic and affirming, but it is also directive. When talking to someone about change, the MI practitioner listens carefully, and gently reinforces any talk of change by reflecting this back to the person, and linking change to the person's core values. By doing this, it points out the discrepancies between the person's behaviour and their own values, for example:

> So on the one hand you're annoyed that people are making a big deal about this, but on the other, there's been a few times you've been worried . . . things have got a bit out of hand, and that's not really how you see yourself.

Its creators, professors of psychology William Miller and Stephen Rollnick (2013), originally developed it through work with problematic alcohol use, and there is now evidence for its use across alcohol, nicotine, drug and gambling addictions, as well as in promoting other areas of positive behaviour change.

Other ways of exploring this ambivalence come from Gestalt and Schema therapeutic models (Nevis, 2000; Young et al., 2003), which open up the internal dialogues that go on when we are in conflict with ourselves, and aim to strengthen the healthier, coping side of ourselves. If our needs are met, we develop into fairly healthy and responsible adults, able to cope with the majority of life's ups and downs without having to hide from, compensate for or submit to raw emotional needs. In brain terms, we have well-developed and adaptive prefrontal cortices. If some emotional needs were not met, we might recognise different facets to our personalities, and sometimes these parts of ourselves may be in conflict with each other. One way of understanding this is to imagine you are facing a decision about whether or not to follow your addictive behaviour. You might have conflicting emotions about this. What happens if you give each of these a voice? What does the frightened part of you need? What about the angry part? Now imagine the part of yourself that you want to be, or if that's too difficult to imagine, think up a wise and compassionate companion, who cares very deeply about you and only wants the best for you. What does this part think that you need?[1]

One potential difficulty with these approaches is that the individual needs a certain amount of awareness and insight into the things driving the addiction. The more unconscious and automatic the drivers, the more likely it is that attempts to change might be derailed once the person is at home and surrounded by the 'sirens' of addiction pulling them towards the old behavioural patterns. Because our reward system very efficiently establishes cues signifying reward as hugely preferential, it's as though our brain says 'yes' to the reward while we are still slowly and consciously deciding what we want to do, even if our conscious decision is 'no'. The stronger this bias, the more likely we are to relapse, unless we can strengthen our resistance to these unconscious urges. How do we manage things that we are not conscious of?

Impulse, compulsion and self-control

As described earlier, when addictive behaviours are automatic, seeking to control your environment as far as possible is a good first step, known as 'stimulus control'. Knowing that there are two processing systems in the brain, the faster 'impulsive' system and the slower 'reflective system', means that we can try to develop techniques that tap into both of these systems in order to change behaviour. The reflective system responds to reason; the impulsive system is more erratic, and jumps in to sort out emotional problems or when it has been signalled by the cues in the environment. The impulsive system is always scanning, like an automatic radar that is always on, looking out for things that are important or significant for us. This is useful, most of the time. We are immersed in information, and if we tried to pay attention to all of it we would be frozen to the spot and overwhelmed (interestingly, this is what appears to happen for people with autism, who don't filter information in the same way as most, exposing them to a maelstrom of emotion, noise and information which leads to sometimes unusual behaviours as a way of maintaining control of what feels like a hurricane). With addictive behaviours, the cues are compelling because they started out so emotionally relevant. To manage them, we need ways of shortcutting the reward system, and training both 'top-down' (reflective) and 'bottom-up' (impulsive) processes, harnessing motivation for recovery just as it has been harnessed for addiction. Our reflective system has limited attention; it's as though our attention is a spotlight which can come under conscious control, but which is taken over and focused by the demands of the impulsive system when it sees something it wants, with the persistence of a toddler who is trying to get your attention. *Look here! Look! Look!* Where our attention is directed dictates what we do, unless we have ways of consciously redirecting attention to where we want it. So how do we train our brain?

One way of 'kicking out' the entrenched addictive behaviour is by giving the reward system some better alternatives, using the same processes of operant conditioning that got us into the mess in the first place. Behavioural interventions provide rewards or encouragements for specified behaviours, and have been used to modify behaviour in many settings, such as through the use of star charts for children. In drug and alcohol treatment, Contingency Management (CM) is an approach built on this idea. For example, we know that people who complete treatment are more likely to stay in recovery, but dropout rates are high. Treatment is frequently challenging, and sometimes it is easier to slide back into old patterns, which means that treatment must use the tools of reward. Rewards are agreed with the person, but studies have included things like vouchers, more flexibility around prescription arrangements, or other forms of support. Contingent rewards have led to people being more likely to stay in treatment, to stick to treatment plans and reduce their substance use (Petry, 2000). We all do things because we want the reward at the end of the work we put in, and even when we know we want it, motivation can falter. Contingency management is highly effective, but its use across services is still patchy as a result of poor political will and media stories about 'rewarding junkies for taking drugs', the subtext once again being that drug addicts are bad, worthless, and should be punished, not rewarded. This is now shifting in some areas because of the strength of the results. The benefits to people with addictions and the communities around them of using evidence-based treatments are clear. Other approaches like the Community Reinforcement Approach integrate systems of reward to alter the person's social environment, so that social networks can begin to reinforce more appropriate and non-addictive behaviours (Smith et al., 2001).

Can we train the brain to find reward cues less attractive? There are research studies which have shown that keeping something in your working memory (your immediate memory, the part that you might use when rehearsing a phone number to remember, for example) helps the 'top-down' processes, focusing attention on a single goal – 'When I get to the party, I will ask for a Coke' – although this strategy may be ineffective if it is faced with a broad net of unconscious cues, falling prey to the 'ego fatigue' described in Chapter 2 (Ryan, 2013). In general, when trying to train your brain to manage impulses, the answers lie in setting clear and achievable goals and keeping it simple. Problem solving training and SMART goal setting (specific, measurable, achievable, realistic and time-limited) are ways of developing goals that gradually move towards a preferred outcome. The key here is the gradual shaping of behaviour, because the more you achieve small goals, the more confidence you feel in taking the next steps, the 'gradualism' described by Scott Kellogg on page 69. Perhaps you have been unemployed for a while, and want to get back to work, knowing that if you did, you would have less time for drinking, and would feel better about yourself. The goal 'get a job' is huge and might seem overwhelming, and the more overwhelmed you feel, the more likely you might be to stick your head back into the sand (or the bottle). If your goals are smaller and more achievable, you will have a greater chance of success. For example, look up the jobs pages and decide which jobs you can apply for. Pick one. Ask a friend to help you fill out the application form. See if there is any voluntary work you can do to get more experience. Set yourself deadlines, so that you know when the goal has been met, for example, 'I will find three jobs to apply for by Sunday'. The same applies to addictive behaviours. The goal 'stop using' is complicated, but the smaller goals of 'have two days out of the week where I don't use, find a self-help group, contact a self-help group, tell someone I need to stop using, find the number of the local drugs service, contact the local drugs service' are all infinitely more achievable, and allow small steps to be taken closer to your goals.

Just knowing how our brains work can also be helpful. Our brains are tricky, and we can sometimes judge ourselves harshly for processes that are automatic and not really under our control. The clinical psychologist Frank Ryan has pointed out that if you are trying to change an addictive behaviour and have noticed how often your attention gets pulled to the cues of addiction – the alcohol aisle in the supermarket, the tinfoil and spoons in someone's kitchen (these can be significant cues for heroin use), the web page of an online gambling forum – this can feel disheartening. 'I'm doing all this work but I still can't ignore it. . . . I must still be addicted. . . . I must still want it if I'm noticing it all the time. . . . I'm going to end up using again. . . . I'm basically still a junkie'. This relentless trail of worry and thoughts about what the 'noticing' means about you and your prospects can wear down willpower and make a relapse more likely. What if instead, when you noticed your attention being pulled towards the object of your addiction, you said to yourself, 'It's OK. It doesn't mean anything. It's just my brain being tricky. I know that I want to change. It doesn't mean I will give in', and gently guided your attention back to where you want it. The preferential processing associated with addictive behaviours is a normal quirk of the reward system, not a sign of your weakening commitment (Ryan, 2013).

This process of training one's attention is at the core of mindfulness meditation, which has been promoted for years (millennia if you go back to the Buddhist teachings) as a way of finding balance and enhancing conscious control. Meditation increases awareness of the processes of mind, and teaches acceptance of your present experience. Through this practice in disengaging from automatic reaction, it counteracts the 'wanting' of our 'hungry ghosts'. It provides a way to step outside the intrusion and compulsion that characterise addictive behaviours. It teaches us to train attention, and every time attention is pulled away, to gently guide it back, as well as to practice awareness of moment-to-moment experience without judgement. This is grounded in an ethos of compassion, so that you don't blame yourself for these reactions, but move towards accepting and detaching from them. The practice of 'being aware of whatever is there', on a background of compassionate curiosity and acceptance, also improves our ability to notice some of the unconscious needs that may be driving the addiction. What does the craving feel like in the body? What thoughts drift through the mind? Sometimes reaching for the food, drug or distraction is a way of avoiding 'whatever is present', and learning alternative ways of meeting those underlying needs brings them under more conscious control.

Thinking about thinking

We know that the processes leading to and maintaining addictive behaviours are influenced by our beliefs and attitudes. Cognitive Behavioural Therapy (CBT) is a therapy designed to make the individual a therapist of their own experience, by observing their behaviour, understanding its triggers (where we are conscious to these), and recognising the influence of thoughts and beliefs. Beliefs about addictive behaviours are important. It might be about our self-efficacy: "I can't do this without drinking" or "I can do this"; our expectations of what the behaviour will give us: "I will feel better . . . I will not feel like this . . . I will be in control . . . I will not feel"; giving ourselves permission: "Once won't hurt . . . I won't take very long . . . I deserve it" (Mitcheson et al., 2010). The way that we think influences how we feel, our physical responses and our behaviour. Patterns of thought are habits just as much as addictive behaviours, and if we are used to our thoughts sliding into particular grooves, this can be hard to shift.

If we feel low, it's as though our thoughts put a negative filter on everything we see, so we tilt towards the pessimistic view of our prospects, our potential, ourselves. If we feel angry, we see injustices and personal slights wherever we look. CBT explores these patterns and the relationships between them, and helps to separate things out. We are not the same as our thoughts or emotions, and taking a step back to challenge them can help us to feel more in control. If you are doing a course of CBT, you and your therapist might set up behavioural experiments to test out particular beliefs. You might think 'I can't go out without a drink – if I do, I won't be able to talk to anyone and everyone will laugh at me. I'll be humiliated', and set up an experiment in which you agree to test it out. You might arm yourself with some ideas about starting a conversation and perhaps some trusted friends to help you out. If you find that your worst fears aren't realised, you will have a huge confidence boost. If the experiment falls flat, it is just as useful, so that you can think about what went wrong and adapt your approach next time. Learning about how our interpretations influence our emotions and behaviour can help us to understand the cycles of addictive behaviour that can keep us trapped.

Addiction and emotion: finding balance

Emotions, like urges and cravings, act like waves, sweeping over us with different levels of intensity and sometimes carrying us away. Addictive behaviours and emotional difficulties might have branched out of the same roots of early adversity, or because long-term exposure to an addictive behaviour has influenced the brain's emotion regulation systems. Remember that when our stress system is on high alert it struggles to think, and it is harder to control impulses. Under increasing pressure, we are all likely to fall back on habitual ways of reacting, so learning emotional control is a vital part of managing addictive behaviours. This is true whether your addictive behaviour has developed as a way of managing emotions, or whether it is your addiction that is playing havoc with your emotions. Drug and alcohol use might depress or heighten emotion, often intensifying the emotions we might be trying to manage. The danger of smoking cannabis to relax and feel less anxious, or using heroin, or drinking alcohol, is that when withdrawal kicks in, anxiety and agitation will increase because of the way that the substances are metabolised. These issues can be a particular problem for people using benzodiazepine drugs like diazepam to cope with anxiety, as tolerance for these drugs builds rapidly, and they start to create rebound symptoms of anxiety and insomnia when withdrawing from your system. If you don't recognise these as withdrawals, you might find yourself trapped in a cycle of taking more of the drugs that are causing your symptoms. If substance use has become a way of avoiding feelings, and has gone on for a long time, experiencing your own emotions can feel like you're 'going mad', because they seem so alien to you. Although this is hard to tolerate, it also provides an opportunity to get to know yourself, learn about how and why you feel this way, and learn to surf these waves.

Recognising how we feel is the first step towards managing emotions, no matter how big the waves feel. We need to learn about what we really feel, and what we really need, because it isn't the object of addiction, no matter how compelling that may seem. Something as simple as labelling an emotion, no matter how overwhelming, can give you a boat to ride out the waves: 'I feel overwhelmed'; 'I'm really anxious'; 'I'm so angry'. It gives you a chance to ask, 'What can I do about this?', rather than feel swept up and blindsided by the emotion. And what can you do about it? Sometimes it's about considering how much control you might have over the situation and deciding what to let go of. Although this can be difficult, turning towards difficulties rather than avoiding them allows you to consider which problems you can tackle, and which to let go of for the time being. Low mood and restlessness may be heightened by boredom and isolation, so giving yourself a schedule, and thinking about activities that give you a sense of pleasure or achievement is useful – it is a strategy known as 'activity scheduling' in therapy terms. These strategies can be enhanced by finding encouraging phrases for yourself to remind you of what you are trying to do in changing things for yourself, such as 'I can manage this, I have survived so much already and I will survive this too'; 'If I eat this I will feel better in the short term, but it will not last. I want to feel better in the long term'. If you can, ask people you trust to give you positive and encouraging statements too, to act as evidence of your own strength when this is hard for you to find yourself.

The practice of 'urge surfing' is drawn from mindfulness, and can be used in response to both cravings and emotions (Marlatt, 2002). This is a useful exercise, particularly if you feel frightened of your emotions and their consequences. It's just about staying with the emotion, not trying to hide from it or change it, accepting it for what it is, and staying with the rise and fall, like a surfer riding a wave. You might fall in every now and then, but that's OK, it's just about the practice, and each time you find the way to balance and surf the wave, you are training your brain to pause before reacting, and showing yourself that you are able to cope. Relaxation strategies, like training your breathing, or finding strategies that soothe your senses (like calming pictures, soothing smells or soft things to touch) are useful ways of teaching yourself to manage the physical manifestations of anxiety and agitation like a racing heart and tension. Art, music and dance may be ways of expressing things that you don't yet have words for. Slowing and deepening your breath triggers your body's parasympathetic nervous system, the antidote to the 'fight or flight' response. Although it might sound easier said than done, if you learn to control your breath, you learn to control your mind. Some of this is just about looking after yourself – talking to yourself gently, making sure that you get enough sleep and that you eat well. Change sometimes starts from the belief that you deserve for things to be better.

MAINTAINING CHANGES

Managing emotions and learning how to control impulses are both key components in changing addictive behaviours, but changing your lifestyle is rarely a smooth process and there are always challenges along the way. Sometimes this might come from those internal unconscious biases, sometimes from external social and cultural pressures not to change. If changing your behaviour involves breaking away from a group that you have been a part of for a long time, the group might resist this 'new you'. The connection between stress and relapse has been explored for decades, most notably by the late, great Professor Alan Marlatt, who along with many colleagues, shifted the view of relapse from the 'don't talk about it or you'll make it happen', to a nuanced and evidence-based programme of understanding the factors that contribute to relapse in order to develop skills to prevent it. This approach is useful not just for addictive behaviours but for other mental health difficulties also. He and his co-researcher Katie Witkiewitz outlined a 'dynamic model of relapse' in 2004, which moves away from understanding relapse as a linear 'this happens and then this happens', to a recognition that there are a number of complex and interacting factors determining whether someone uses or doesn't use in any given moment (Witkiewitz and Marlatt, 2004). Recovery is rarely a smooth road: change tends to happen gradually, although the complexity of the system leaves room for the stories of people who just wake up one day and stop for good.

To move away from any addictive behaviour, life without the addiction needs to be fulfilling and rewarding. We know from Chapter 3 that people whose lives have been a struggle from their earliest days are more likely to seek less healthy ways of coping with them. Finding some pleasure and purpose in life is a way of ensuring that the pull of the addictive behaviour will be met by a stronger pull from secure relationships, purposeful activity, a robust sense of self-esteem, and a life worth living. It is about building 'recovery capital', the internal and external resources that are required to make and maintain changes (White and Cloud, 2008). Changing addictive behaviours may involve a shift in identity, more profound if the addictive behaviour started when young. Even for those whose brains have been more significantly affected by long-term drug or alcohol use and the self-neglect and poor health that builds up alongside this, some change is possible, although more external help may be required. Alan Marlatt and his team recognised that if change is to be sustained, it must be a long-term process, and access to support should continue beyond the weeks or months usually offered by treatment services. This is where social and community support can be crucial, providing a safety net to catch and consolidate those steps to change, strengthening and supporting a person's new healthier identity.

5

SAFETY IN NUMBERS

Nourishing the hungry ghosts

Relationships are the key to recovery from addiction, so much so that introducing even one sober person to someone's network following alcohol detoxification reduces their likelihood of relapse by 27% (Litt et al., 2007). We develop and adapt our identities in connection with those around us whose opinions we value and whose judgement we trust, writing and re-writing the stories we tell about ourselves. To find the space between urge or craving and action, we need to imagine a future self that is more valuable than the immediate reward, to make the story of our potential, non-addicted lives more compelling. So how can we use relationships to facilitate recovery, in small-scale ways within families and friendship groups, and on a larger scale, in communities and societies? Our local social groups play a huge part in setting the parameters of acceptable behaviour, and can either limit or encourage addictive behaviours, further influenced by our location, setting, and the availability of substances. Many groups have been formed from people coming together to try and support and learn from each other, and one of the best known when we are talking about addiction recovery is Alcoholics Anonymous (AA).

THE POWER OF A FELLOWSHIP

AA began in 1935 in Ohio (US), when Bill Wilson and Dr Bob Smith met and used ideas of fellowship from their own recoveries to develop the 12 steps that still form the basis of AA's philosophy and methods (AA, 2001). Originally, AA saw addiction as a mental and spiritual 'malady', but later adopted the disease model. It was set up to offer mutual support through bringing together people who want to stop drinking, and by encouraging this through shared experience, honesty and working through the steps. You are the expert on your own experience, and all you have to do is turn up. It was groundbreaking in its recognition that people addicted to alcohol needed help, not judgement, and that recovery was possible. To get there, you need to admit your essential powerlessness in the face of your addiction, recognise that you have a lifelong disease because of a personal vulnerability to alcohol, and see abstinence as the only option. You are asked to trust in a higher authority, but this can be anything you choose. By accepting help, you work towards then being able to help others. There is no hierarchy. Groups are organised and facilitated by members, and new members are encouraged to seek out a 'sponsor' (someone further down the road of recovery, whose recovery 'you want') to mentor them through their first meetings and help them to attend.

The 12 steps were adapted to support those with narcotics addictions (NA in the 1950s), and has since grown to develop support groups for cocaine (Cocaine Anonymous), gambling (Gamblers Anonymous), compulsive eating (Overeaters Anonymous) and family members of a person struggling with addiction (Al-Anon), all based on the 12-step model. Addiction isolates and shames, so the supportive network provided by 12-step fellowships may be someone's first, and sometimes only, safe and non-judgemental social network. Some of the 12-step components mirror ideas from Cognitive Behavioural Therapy (CBT) and relapse prevention, such as looking at how thinking influences behaviour, known as 'stinking thinking' in the fellowships. The repetition and predictable structure of groups provide an effective way of creating new habits, and also provide a form of rehabilitation for those in early recovery from drug and alcohol addiction who may find it hard to remember, plan and problem solve effectively at first. The openness of groups to people at every stage of recovery offer exposure to the hope of recovery, as well as lived examples of the potential traps and challenges. Participating regularly – and you are encouraged to attend 30 meetings in 30 days at the beginning – ensures that your goal of abstinence is held in mind and reinforced with every meeting. Twelve-step groups have helped millions of people to get their lives back on track. They have paved the way for a host of other mutual aid and self-help groups, such as Self-Management and Recovery Training (SMART Recovery), a group which uses principles of CBT to teach coping skills, and is open to anyone seeking to change any addictive or compulsive behaviour, without necessarily specifying a goal of abstinence. SMART Recovery also offers online groups, which can be vital for those unable to reach meetings (UK Smart Recovery, 2016). The range of self-help options now available ensures choice for people seeking a supportive group, whatever their initial goals may be.

Although an essential part of a system promoting recovery, there are pros and cons to self-help groups, and it is useful to be fully informed of these. The psychologist Stanton Peele says of AA, "the best that we can say about AA is that it works for those for whom it works" (Peele et al., 1992, pp. 19–46). The available evidence on effectiveness of AA is mixed, although some evidence shows higher rates of abstinence for those that attend regularly. A thorough review of the evidence carried out in 2006 found no convincing evidence of effectiveness (Ferri et al., 2006). AA's adoption of the disease model has led to extreme views in some groups: if you don't buy in to a 12-step approach, or even if you do and you relapse, it's your fault. You didn't follow the steps. You're making excuses if you talk about your reasons for drinking or using. You didn't try hard enough. And back we go to the moralising of the nineteenth century. Without a supportive group structure, the steps can be punitive, and promote the idea that people experiencing addiction need to 'hit rock bottom' before having enough of an incentive to change, despite many people having faced repeated traumas.

Maia Szalawitz points out that "the reality is that 'bottom' is a narrative device in a story of sin and redemption, not a medical description of a key stage in recovery from addictions" (2016, p. 184). Recovery is enhanced when treatments are empathic and empowering, and there are many routes to recovery, both within and outside the 12-step fellowships. Fellowships and other self-help groups are also as varied as they are numerous, and as with any groups, problems can arise. Sexual exploitation has been highlighted so frequently that it has been termed the '13th step', when a person in early recovery is seduced by someone with a longer length of sobriety or stability. Groups can also be used as marketing opportunities for drug dealers seeking to access new customers, exposing vulnerable people to further harm, although many groups are able to pick up these issues and deal with them quickly and effectively. If you are considering attending a 12-step or other type of self-help group, it is useful to visit a few, and speak to different people about their experiences, before deciding on a group and sponsor that you trust and can engage with.

Caveats aside, 12-step, self-help and peer support groups are integral to a system that supports recovery. Some of the difficulties of 12-step groups may be a result of their dominance in the addiction 'treatment' field, which has led to their adoption by many specialist treatment services. Twelve-step groups are not therapies, and their proponents are not therapists. They were never supposed to be. Their strength is in their openness to all, their sharing of personal experience and the supportive networks that they provide for people, for as long as they might need them. No specialist service can offer that. People finding their way to the groups for the first time may never have experienced such acceptance and support, and the strength of this connection and the hope that it provides is incalculable. Their emphasis on helping others to recover also influenced the creation of peer support groups, who can act as invaluable bridges between treatment services and the community, offering visible examples of hope and possibility (White, 2009). As the Buddhist teacher Thich Nhat Hanh says, "We have to build community a little bit everywhere so these hungry ghosts can find refuge" (Thich Nhat Hanh, 2007).

A FAMILY AFFAIR

There is an anecdotal figure often quoted for drug and alcohol addiction that says that for each person with an addiction, four others are significantly affected. This includes parents, siblings, partners and friends; the people who pick up the pieces, clean up the messes, suffer the loss, anger and pain, or unfortunately in some cases add to the toxicity. Worldwide, a very conservative estimate suggests that 100 million adults could be affected by a relative's addiction problems, bringing increased stress, ill health and a global personal and economic burden (Orford et al., 2013). Family-focused self-help groups have been developed, such as Al-Anon and Gam-Anon (for family members of people with alcohol and gambling problems), and a range of psychological interventions have been designed to try to meet family's needs.

There is a family training component to the Community Reinforcement Approach, which trains family members to reinforce non-addictive behaviours, with a specific emphasis on supporting drug users into treatment (Meyers et al., 1999). There are also interventions that work with whole families, or social networks, such as Family Therapy, or Social Behavioural Network Therapy (SBNT; Copello et al., 2002). These recognise that we are more likely to be able to change, and maintain changes, if we have a strong social network encouraging and supporting us. In order to strengthen the network, SBNT offers training in a range of techniques, such as communication and coping skills, and planning for 'slips' and relapses that consider the whole social or family network.

In some disease-focused interventions, the family's attempts to help can be criticised as 'enabling' the addiction or encouraging co-dependence. Most often, family members are ordinary people trying to cope with a complex and highly stressful situation, and addictive behaviours are disempowering to everyone caught up in them. This underlies the Stress-Strain-Coping-Support Framework developed by Jim Orford and his colleagues, which steps away from blaming family members for difficulties, instead offering them a way to take back responsibility and control for their situation (Orford et al., 2010). The model recognises that families and individuals with addictive behaviours will typically do their best to cope with stressful situations, but if coping strategies don't work, the strain on the family increases, leading to all sorts of health problems and poor mental health. The model has led to a deceptively simple intervention, known as the '5-Step Method'. The five steps involve looking at a family's particular needs, providing information, exploring family responses and coping strategies, enhancing social support and looking at other forms of assistance that might be useful. It emphasises that addiction places the family members under significant stress in their own right, and so improving family coping more generally improves things for both family members and the person with the addiction. It is flexible enough that it has been adapted to multiple different settings worldwide, and has had promising results across different countries and cultural groups, from Mexican rural indigenous communities to majority white and minority Muslim groups in England (Copello et al., 2010).

Each family might need different ways of coping with a dysfunctional situation, and what's right for one might be terrible for another. Doing something such as buying alcohol for a partner who wants it to stave off their withdrawals has been judged as 'enabling the addiction'. But what if the partner might become angry and unpredictable without the alcohol? Is it the better option to protect yourself and your children? Each strategy will have pros and cons in particular situations, and the 5-Step Method provides a way of exploring this, as well as providing specific information to empower and inform the family member, and support safety for the whole family.

What about when there are children in the family? Having a parent who uses drugs or drinks excessively doesn't automatically affect parenting or place children at risk, but it does make it more likely that there could be problems, and it does increase the risk of violence. As you may remember from Chapter 3, problematic drug or alcohol use can create 'adverse early life experiences' for children, because it makes it harder for parents to provide a nurturing and predictable environment. The impact can also be in utero: children whose mothers are unable to stop drinking alcohol while they are pregnant are at risk of developing Foetal Alcohol Spectrum Disorders (FASD), which can result in learning difficulties, as well as a host of other behavioural and physical problems. Figures suggest that around 8.3 million children in the US live with a parent with an addiction (FADA, 2013), and in the UK there are up to 3.85 million children who live with at least one parent using alcohol or drugs problematically (ACMD, 2011; Manning et al., 2009). Addiction skews priorities, and sometimes this means that the most important parts of life are sidelined as attention and resources are focused on the object of desire. To a child, this can be bewildering and immensely painful. Research exploring the experiences of children living in these situations tells us that it can feel like there is an elephant in the room, "a huge and dominating presence impossible for children to ignore" (Kroll, 2003, p. 132), but which is often ignored, minimised or denied. There may be experiences of loss, grief, shame, resentment and anger, and in situations of abuse or violence there may be pervasive fear. In these situations, children are forced to grow up too quickly, sometimes ending up caring for adults struggling to care for themselves, with their own emotional and physical needs sometimes going unmet. Where help is available, it can be difficult for children to talk about what is happening, out of a wish to protect and remain loyal to their parent(s), or out of fear that their family will be broken up. They may need a safe and trusting relationship in order to be able to open up about what is happening at home, with awareness of how information will be used, and the possible implications of this. Well-resourced and well-trained staff in schools, children's and social services, with time to spend building relationships with children and families, can offer connection, safety and support, and prevent a situation deteriorating whenever possible.

HOW SOCIETY SOWS THE SEEDS OF ADDICTION

Families are influenced by the communities and societies in which they are embedded, and as we know, brain development is intrinsically social. We respond to social pressure from authority and from our peers. In societies where violence against women is normal, even acceptable, it occurs much more frequently. Where it is unacceptable and criminalised, the frequency drops sharply. In cultures where alcohol is prohibited for religious reasons, such as in the Mormon church or the Muslim religion, rates of alcohol abstinence tend to be above 70% (Michalak et al., 2007). From Chapter 3, we know that addictive behaviours are more likely to set seed in someone who has been neglected or deprived of nurturing, but can also develop as a result of repetition and opportunity, particularly in environments which encourage excess. Problematic drug and alcohol use does seem to be more likely in certain communities, such as areas of high deprivation, some immigrant and indigenous groups. Does this mean that there are groups of people who are more likely to become addicted? Aboriginal groups in Australia have twice the rates of alcohol addiction than the rest of the population. Is it just that they have different genes and are more susceptible? Hopefully at this point you will know that the answer is a resounding no.

There are some genetic differences in the way that alcoholism is metabolised among certain groups. Some East Asian people are hypersensitive to even small amounts of alcohol and develop what is sometimes known as the 'flushing syndrome'. It is a bit like an allergic reaction to alcohol, causing nausea, headaches, sweating, palpitations and the blushing which gives it its name. People with this genetic vulnerability tend to avoid alcohol as it makes them feel terrible, but the power of peer pressure sometimes overcomes this, and there are anecdotal reports of young people taking antihistamines before drinking as a way of counteracting the effects in order to drink with their friends. The flushing response is caused by two genetic mutations, one that leads to alcohol being broken down much more quickly into its metabolite acetaldehyde, and the other which breaks down acetaldehyde much more slowly. This is dangerous news for those who do continue to drink despite their uncomfortable reaction, because acetaldehyde is much more toxic than alcohol, and people with these mutations have a higher risk of oesophageal cancer and digestive tract problems (Brooks et al., 2009). This is an unfortunate example of how social and cultural factors might outweigh a genetic tendency to avoid alcohol.

However, there are no genetic vulnerabilities among indigenous populations that explain the increased frequencies of addictive behaviours. Before the Europeans arrived, there was no alcohol use among Indigenous Canadians and New Zealand Maori, and limited use by Australian Aboriginal people. After the arrival of the European colonists who effectively introduced alcohol to Australia, use among the Aboriginal people increased to similar levels to that seen among the colonists themselves (Saggers and Gray, 1998). The dispossession, disease, forced moves of different tribal groups to reservations, social exclusion, trauma, poverty and racism destroyed much of the social connection and culture of the Aboriginal people, and of course contributed to the harmful use of alcohol. The 'stolen generation', the group of Aboriginal people who, as children, were legally and forcibly removed from their families, are twice as likely to use alcohol and drugs in harmful ways (Zubrick et al., 2004). The profound losses endured by indigenous populations, the breakdown and destruction of the narrative of cultural identity, all left a gaping hole often filled by alcohol and drugs, making it more likely that the next generation would also grow up traumatised. There are higher rates of mental health problems, suicide, physical and social problems among some groups of indigenous populations, although not all. Those communities that have preserved and restored cultural traditions, and gained control over services such as for health and education, show lower rates of suicide and poor mental health, and better rates of recovery from addictive behaviours (Chandler and Lalonde, 2008).

Our stress response systems were primed to respond to physical and social threats thousands of years ago, only now many more of the threats that we face are complex and nuanced. Moving from indigenous groups to deprived communities in the UK, there are parallels in the loss of purpose, loss of a community narrative and traditions, loss of work and displacement. There are similarities in the difficulties faced globally by people who have been "expelled from society, lack agency and play no active role in the economic system beyond casting fear on those inside it" (Standing, 2015, p. 2). Although this might sound a little dramatic, research shows that being at the bottom of the social ladder triggers our stress response systems, and if this happens for too long a period of time, we endure harsh consequences to our physical and mental health (Marmot, 2006).The highest levels of stress come from situations in which we have the lowest amount of control and autonomy over our lives: our stress systems are mediated by our social systems.

WE ARE NOT BORN EQUAL

The destruction caused by addictive behaviours, particularly to drugs and alcohol, is not equitably distributed. Globally, people at the lower rungs of the socioeconomic spectrum consume less alcohol than those higher up the social scale, and are actually more likely to abstain from alcohol, but experience worse health consequences, like liver disease, or early death (WHO, 2014). In the UK, the less money you have, the more likely you are to die from alcohol-related causes, particularly for men, and particularly in Scotland (Scottish Government, 2008). Drug use in general is more likely if you live in a deprived area, but use of class A drugs (drugs seen as more dangerous under UK drug policy, including heroin, methadone, cocaine, ecstasy, LSD and magic mushrooms) is fairly equally distributed across socioeconomic groups (Home Office, 2015). It's the consequences that are most problematic. If you are from a deprived background and use drugs, you are more likely to use problematically, take more risks (such as injecting drugs), start using at a younger age, have more criminal involvement (though remember that you are more likely to pick up drug-related charges if you are poor or non-white, even when there are similar levels of drug use), and end up with more health and social complications as a result of your drug use (Galea and Vlakov, 2002). In some communities, problematic drug use can seem inescapable and entrenched. Growing up in a deprived environment can also affect brain development, because children may have less exposure to complex language and enriched activities. Exposure to poverty in early life has been described as a significant risk factor for poor developmental outcomes, although as with many of the risk factors outlined in this chapter, this risk is mitigated by nurturing and responsive caregiving (Luby et al., 2013).

Why might there be more problematic drug use in a deprived community? Along with deprivation come potential threats of unemployment or precarious employment, insecure housing, poor familial health, choices between food and heat. The knowledge that you're not able to provide the nurturing and responsive caregiving that you want to give your children, because of your level of stress. There is the additional pressure of the stigma that targets those forced into poverty, as illustrated by politically driven media campaigns attacking people receiving welfare support, which have resurrected Victorian definitions of 'undeserving' and 'deserving' poor. Whenever the pressures start mounting, our threat systems shut down our reflective systems and we start reacting more quickly, making more decisions under pressure, and adopting a 'just get on with it' approach; the coping strategy of many who have few options from which to choose. You don't think, you can't plan, and it's harder to think creatively when you're living from day to day. When this happens to whole communities, they suffer as a whole. Bruce Perry and Maia Szalawitz point out that societies enduring great traumas, such as war or oppression, cannot flourish, because "just as children grow up as a reflection of the developmental environment provided by their parents and immediate family, so does the inventiveness, creativity and productivity of a people reflect the developmental environment of their society" (Szalavitz and Perry, 2010, p. 117). Across the UK, the de-industrialisation policies of the 1980s left entire communities facing unemployment, at a time when the availability of drugs was also increasing dramatically. This created a perfect storm from which many communities are still recovering (Foster, 2000).

Thirty years after 'Rat Park', Bruce Alexander published an account of how addiction spreads in response to the dislocation and individualism promoted by free-market economics and capitalism. These prioritise profits and growth over social capital, or the value of trusting and connected social networks. He gives a convincing argument that the fracturing of cultural and social connections has damaged our 'psychosocial integration', leaving us powerless and disconnected. This lack of connection leaves a void of unfulfilled need that advertising companies and retail organisations pour images and products and brands into without pause. Consumerism loves addiction. We need more, must have more, and can never be satisfied with what we have. Although you could argue that addiction itself leads to fragmentation of communities, damaging families and perpetuating problems, historical accounts of the spread of addiction across societies offer a compelling counterargument that addiction comes as a consequence of societal disempowerment and dislocation, rather than a cause (Alexander, 2008; Hart, 2013b).

BUILDING BRIDGES

So how do we build communities that promote social cohesion and recovery? Research from many disciplines has converged on the understanding that the stronger the social networks within a society, the more resilient the society. Countries that have smaller gaps between the poorest and richest (the most economically equal) are more cohesive.[1] This has far-reaching implications, and not just when considering addictive behaviours. Society creates the context in which recovery can occur. If society marginalises people with addictions, seeing them as 'separate' and 'other', it can only exacerbate and entrench the problem, by reducing the choices available to those defined under that label. Reduction and prevention of addiction at a population level needs a shift right across the social spectrum. Part of this is through recognising that in more equal societies we are all better off. Less equal societies are less stable, because people at opposite ends of the social spectrum find it increasingly harder to find common ground and identify with each other, reducing empathy and the sense that 'we are all in it together'. As trust is eroded, we become more disconnected and fragmented. The better off see the worse off as 'lazy scroungers', and the worse off see the better off as 'out-of-touch elites who have rigged the system'. And if the system is rigged, why vote? Why obey the social rules? This was demonstrated by the research of Richard Wilkinson and Kate Pickett, who showed that rich but unequal countries do worse than poorer, but more equal, countries on a whole host of measures. With greater income inequality, crime, corruption and tribalism increase. Physical health, mental health and life satisfaction decrease. This isn't just about the people at the bottom rungs of the ladder; it's about the kind of society we all want to live in. And it isn't just about drugs and alcohol; the addictions at the higher echelons of the socioeconomic spectrum – to money, power and endless economic growth – are widening the gap between the rich and the poor exponentially, and compounding the social difficulties described here.

We can't change society overnight, but how can we start building the connections between each other and our communities? The answers lie back where we started at the beginning of this chapter, in the hope and determination that emerge from communities of people coming together to build a shared narrative, such as with the 12-step fellowships, with peer support groups, or with other recovery communities globally. The group provides scaffolding for the individuals within it to develop a shared identity and belonging, soothing the threat of disconnection through social connection, and enabling growth and development. It is strong communities that nourish hungry ghosts.

Stronger communities can be supported by psychological, social and medical treatment services, but in many ways these services are there to help people develop their own helpful and healthy relationships. It is these relationships which offer our most important stress relief system. Services remain very focused on the individual, although the recovery movement has swept through many treatment systems, demanding that they open up and build bridges with communities of empowered and inspiring people in recovery. As they say, recovery is contagious. There is a need for a balance between recovery communities and treatment services, in order to ensure that the richness of lived experience and 'what worked for me' can be integrated (and not confused) with the evidence and research of treatment systems and 'what works for many'.

In the case of drug and alcohol addiction, this can only be done by considering interventions at different stages of individual development, and at multiple societal levels, from individual responsibility to public policy.

6

MAKE LOVE NOT WAR

If drug policy understood the science of compassion

At the beginning of this book we learned that addiction can be defined as any compulsive behaviour, pursued despite negative consequences. We also learned that prohibition-based drug policies have grown out of historical racism and marginalisation, actively seeking out and disproportionately punishing people from ethnic minorities and with lower socioeconomic status. If punishment doesn't work, what does? How do we impose some control, while not getting in the way of individual freedoms?

When we talk about drug policy, we inevitably come up against the questions of decriminalisation and legalisation. There is a spectrum of possible approaches here, from full prohibition to full legalisation, with many options in the grey area in between. The argument quickly gets polarised, and is an emotional one. Too many people have lost loved ones to addiction, and we fear exposing our children to drugs in the way that they are currently exposed to alcohol in most Western countries. Alcohol use is often highlighted as an example of what can go wrong when a potentially addictive substance is legal and widely available, and for good reason. The World Health Organization cites alcohol as being at least partially responsible for over 5% of the global burden of disease and injury across the world (WHO, 2014). In fact, when Professor David Nutt and members of the Independent Scientific Committee on Drugs (ISCD, a UK-based advisory committee) carried out an assessment of the relative harms of substances used recreationally in the UK, they found alcohol to be the most harmful drug of all, when taking into account harms to individual users, to others, and to society (Nutt et al., 2010). Interestingly, Professor Nutt was invited to chair this group after being fired from his role as the chair of the UK government–affiliated Advisory Council on the Misuse of Drugs in 2009 by the then Home Secretary Alan Johnson, for stating that cannabis, ecstasy and LSD were less harmful than tobacco and alcohol. Although independent scientific advice is still seen as controversial, its evidence is essential if we are to move toward the development of a credible drug and alcohol strategy.

IS PROHIBITING SUBSTANCES EFFECTIVE?

If alcohol is the most harmful substance around, and it is completely legal, how can we consider legalisation of other drugs? As mentioned in Chapter 1, we have a model of alcohol prohibition from the US between 1919 and 1933 to show us what happened. There were some successes. With reduced access and availability in some corners of society, alcohol use diminished, as did liver disease and deaths attributable to alcohol. However, these modest gains were swamped by the incredible costs. Many people did not want to stop drinking alcohol (archaeological records suggest that humans have been fermenting beverages since the Stone Age, around 12,000 years ago), and this demand left a vacancy filled rapidly by organised criminal gangs. The murder rate in America doubled during the time of alcohol prohibition, and then dropped off sharply after prohibition was repealed (Miron, 1999). Both crime and incarceration rates increased. Prohibiting alcohol also ensured that what was released onto the market was stronger, because for a criminal gang, it is more cost-effective to transport the most alcohol in the smallest space. It gives you more bang for your buck. It also made it much more dangerous to drink alcohol, because you couldn't always tell what you were drinking, and alcohol poisoning during the prohibition era was rife.

Many of these costs of prohibition are still being seen in the 'War on Drugs', described by journalist and author Johann Hari in his book *Chasing the Scream* (2015). Drug production and distribution show no signs of reducing, with no discernible impact on drug consumption, if you look across different drug types and age groups in Europe. Cannabis and cocaine use is fluctuating, MDMA use is increasing, amphetamine use is fairly stable, and although the use of new psychoactive substances is still low, it is causing increasing problems, particularly in marginalised populations (EMCDDA, 2017a). So if the point of drug prohibition is to reduce consumption and limit availability of drugs, it isn't working. As with alcohol, drug prohibition has led to increased dangers for those that do use, because unless you have access to drug testing facilities, it is impossible to be sure what street drugs contain, and they are frequently adulterated as a way of increasing the profit margins and to manage unstable supply chains. It is also impossible for most users to test the potency of street drugs, and their variability can be lethal. Those who habitually use a particular drug will tend to dose themselves according to their previous habits, so if a drug suddenly increases in strength they are at risk of an unintentional overdose. Hospital admissions due to drug use, and drug-related deaths in Europe, have continued to increase (EMCDDA, 2017a). This is about drug use, not necessarily addiction, and the majority of these overdoses are accidental according to the figures. There is so much pain in these statistics. Each death is a member of a family, and the grief and confusion wrought by a drug-related death is sometimes difficult to acknowledge for those left behind, in part due to the ongoing stigma around drug use. If the point of drug prohibition is to reduce drug-related harms, it isn't working.

Along with prohibition and the War on Drugs come harsh sentencing laws for drug-related crimes. This makes sense if we focus on the large-scale organised criminal distribution and manufacture, but is less rational when we look at smaller-scale possession and use. The economist Jeffrey Miron pointed out the obvious, that criminal gangs can't resolve disputes through appealing to courts, so they turn to violence (Miron, 1999). If any form of trade is prohibited while there is ongoing demand for it, it will be regulated through violent means, with the ripples extending out into society, an obvious target for policing. But what about sentencing for individual drug use and possession? Globally, drug possession makes up 83% of all drug-related offences (UNODC, 2015). Does sentencing these offences reduce harm, or reduce harmful drug use? Actually, it does the opposite. At best, there are no differences in the reoffending rates between those who are jailed and those who receive community options, and at worst, there may be an increase in criminal activity following a custodial sentence (Villettaz et al., 2014). This is particularly the case for young offenders, especially those placed in adult facilities. This should come as no surprise from what we know about the way young people use the groups around them to consolidate their identities (Lambie and Randell, 2013). There is no relationship between the severity of drug sentencing laws and rates of drug use (Home Office, 2014). Prison cannot increase recovery capital. Instead it does the opposite, by cutting off many of the connections to positive social relationships, education, employment and secure housing that the individual might otherwise have had. It also enhances isolation and marginalisation. In addition, the weeks after prison release are among the most risky periods of time for overdose, as people are suddenly surrounded by old addictive behaviour cues, with a markedly lower tolerance for using. If drug prohibition and its resulting harsh sentencing laws are trying to reduce drug use, they are not working.

SO IF PROHIBITION DOESN'T WORK, WHAT DOES?

When we are considering decriminalisation and legalisation of substances, it is difficult to use alcohol as an example because of the obvious harms that it causes. But actually, alcohol isn't a great example of how substances could be legalised responsibly, as attempts to regulate the alcohol industry have been met with significant lobbying to prevent this. For example, Scotland's attempts to bring in a minimum price per unit of alcohol (recognised as an evidence-based measure to reduce access to alcohol when used as one of a package of measures) were passed by Ministers in 2012, but are yet to be implemented in 2017 due to legal challenges led by the Scottish Whisky Association who say that it won't work and will damage the industry. So if full prohibition and minimally regulated legalisation aren't ideal, where is the middle ground? One example comes from another legal and highly addictive drug, for which regulation has increased markedly over recent decades, with some interesting consequences.

If you were brought up in the seventies or eighties, you might remember smoking carriages on trains, a smoking area on airplanes, tobacco advertising everywhere, and smoking appearing as an endlessly cool habit thanks to portrayals in TV shows and films. Fast-forward to the present day, when tobacco advertising has been banned, cigarettes are taxed heavily, cigarette packets carry warnings and graphic images about the negative health impacts, public spaces are smoke-free, and tobacco companies have had to pay compensation to people who developed lung cancer, and to cover the costs of treatment for smoking-related diseases, after internal reports were released showing that (of course) they were well aware of the harmful consequences of smoking, but concealed this for decades (ASH, 2017). Although the 'War against Tobacco' is still being waged, it has had many victories. Cigarette smoking in the UK has been halved since the 1970s, and currently stands at about 16% of the population (ONS, 2016). Cigarette smoking worldwide has steadily declined. And increased support (and funding) for stop-smoking campaigns and clinics has been shown to be reasonably effective (Bauld et al., 2009). Could these approaches work for illicit drugs?

In recognition of the failures and huge personal and societal costs of the War on Drugs, countries around the world began to experiment with decriminalisation, alongside the promotion of treatment and rehabilitation instead of incarceration. The first country to take this step was Portugal, which decriminalised all drugs in 2001, removing any penalties for personal-level possession (defined as possessing up to ten days' supply for personal use), although manufacture and supply remain criminal offences. Funds were channelled into an expansion of social and health responses to problematic drug use and addiction. Significantly, the Portuguese government also agreed to subsidise the wages of ex-drug users following treatment for a period of one year to help them back into employment, and to reintegrate with mainstream life. So 16 years later, what happened? Was there an explosion in drug use? In fact, drug use didn't change much between 2001 and 2007, and it actually declined in the group most at risk, those aged 15–24. Injecting drug use halved, and overdose reduced significantly, thought in part to be due to the reduction of social stigma around drug use, and easier access to drug treatment and harm reduction services.

Although there have been conflicting accounts of the reform, careful analysis of the figures found that "evidence-informed conclusions provide ample indication of a successful reform" (Stevens and Hughes, 2012, p. 12). This wasn't just about decriminalisation; accounts of the reform have emphasised the importance of the social policy and welfare changes that accompanied it, and we know that drug penalties tend to bear little relationship to drug use, whether punitive or lenient. The chairman of the Portuguese Institute on Drugs and Drug Addiction, João Goulão, said "the biggest effect has been to allow the stigma of drug addiction to fall, to let people speak clearly and to pursue professional help without fear" (Hawkes, 2011). They succeeded in shifting public opinion away from drug users being 'bad' towards drug users being in need of (and deserving of) support. About 20 countries around the world are now moving towards more liberal approaches to drug policy, with decriminalisation of cannabis use in many. Increasing access to treatment, opportunities to work and reducing stigma all increase the recovery capital required to make and sustain changes. And as these indicators grow and sustain someone's life, there is less of a need for the substance. All of these shifts toward more compassionate, health-focused drug policies, and the mounting evidence in their favour, led the World Health Organization and United Nations to issue a joint statement in June 2017 placing punitive drug policies firmly in the realm of discrimination. They called for states to reduce discrimination, in part by "reviewing and repealing punitive laws that have been proven to have negative health outcomes and that counter established public health evidence. These include laws that criminalize or otherwise prohibit . . . drug use or possession of drugs for personal use" (WHO/UN, 2017).

Some countries have gone even further than decriminalisation. Legalisation of cannabis has been introduced in a number of places, including Uruguay and 30 US states, where most allow consumption for medicinal purposes. There hasn't been a vast outbreak of marijuana use, and estimates suggest that use has remained consistent. Arrests and court cases have been reduced, and income from sales and taxation is in the millions of dollars (UNODC, 2016). These are controversial moves, and there is still resistance to legalising other substances. The dominant story of drugs as monstrous and frightening substances remains, and makes it difficult to see past our fears to a reasoned approach. This is understandable. We see the worst of the consequences of drug use and addiction, because most of the time, the media lens of drug use is focused on the 10% of problematic use and its consequences. So when we try and look at legalisation of all substances from an impartial and reasoned perspective, our fears creep in, stoked by reports of the prescribed opiate epidemic in the US, or the 'ice' (crystalline methamphetamine, a purified version of methamphetamine) epidemic in Australia, and we fear a catastrophe.

IS LEGALISATION OF DRUGS REALLY A GOOD IDEA?

Transform Drug Policy Foundation, an international think tank seeking strict regulation of the drug trade, sees legalisation as a way of establishing effective systems to regulate all drugs, using the evidence base around reducing drug-related harms (TDPF, 2009). Is this really possible? Wouldn't it just send a message that it's 'OK to use', placing more people at risk? The decades of evidence show that we are at greater risk from prohibition than we are from legalisation, provided that appropriate regulations are imposed on how and where particular substances can be used. We worry that legalising drugs will lead to more people using, but we know that this is a misleading indicator of progress. Just as when alcohol prohibition led to greater access to stronger alcoholic drinks, drug prohibition has led to increased availability of more potent substances, and it is hoped that people would move to less harmful substances if they were going to continue to use, such as moving from alcohol to cannabis use. Early research on this is mixed, with evidence of cannabis being used as a preferred substitute for alcohol following legalisation, other evidence that liberal policies lead to increases in both alcohol and cannabis use, and other research finding no significant effect (Guttmannova et al., 2016). It is plausible that problematic drug use and addiction would also decrease, as when substance use is not criminalised it is clearer across society that support for problematic use is the best response. This makes it easier for people to come forward sooner if they are concerned about their use, as there is less stigma and easier access to unbiased help.

The late author and drug war analyst Charles Bowden pointed out that there is a war *on* drugs, which is waged against the substances and those that use them, and a war *for* drugs, which is the violent tussle among criminal gangs to control the trade (Bowden, 2011). Legalisation neatly removes the drug trade from the hands of the cartels, and means that trade agreements are made through negotiation rather than violence. In an interview in 1991, the economist Milton Friedman estimated that drug prohibition caused 10,000 homicides every year (Treback et al., 1992). His view was that he would prefer to regulate drugs in the same way that alcohol and tobacco are regulated, but 26 years after his interview, the Transform Drug Policy Foundation has pointed out that unfettered free trade would be just as damaging, as the consequences of minimally regulated alcohol demonstrate. Their recommendations are based on appraisals of the relative harms of substances, so an expansion of the legally regulated markets to include less harmful drugs, and potential expansion of regulation around more potent substances around potential for medical use. They have illustrated this clearly in the graph below, presented with their permission (see Figure 6.1).[1]

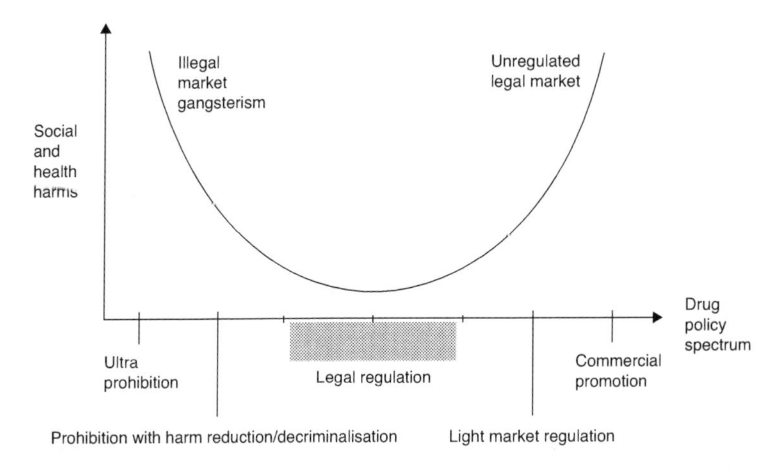

Figure 6.1 The spectrum of policy options available and their likely effects

Strict regulation gives us control. It's currently easier for young people to buy drugs in some areas than it is for them to buy alcohol, because dealers don't ask for ID. Indeed, some young people might be drawn into dealing to their friends as an easy way to make some money, particularly if they have a lack of access to other opportunities. More control ensures regulation of 'set and setting', with some proposed regulations including restricting promotion, availability and imposing age limits. More control means fewer overdoses, because people know what they are taking, and they know that it will be consistent. It also opens up drug uses for medicinal purposes, which is more difficult under strict prohibition. Many drugs that are illegal for recreational use have valuable medicinal qualities, such the existing uses of medical heroin, or diamorphine, being used for severe pain relief in hospitals. There are interesting studies going on currently investigating the use of MDMA, known as ecstasy, to use in combination with psychotherapy to treat post-traumatic stress disorder and other mental health difficulties, because of its ability to increase feelings of trust and compassion (Sessa and Nutt, 2015).

Ending the War on Drugs provides a chance to 'bear witness' to the traumas that it has caused, the first step in beginning reparations and healing. It reduces the demonisation of drugs and brings them back under the category of any behaviour with potential harms or risks associated. The criminalisation of drug use has placed drug users in an 'antisocial' category, enhancing the 'othering' of people that choose to use, and sometimes get trapped in it. And from what we know about drugs and drug use, if someone uses in a self-destructive way, those tendencies are not a property of the drug, but a combination of the drug, the environment, and the particular individual's susceptibility. Bruce Alexander wrote that "fanatical devotion to socially destructive ideas can be a desperate attempt to adapt to severe dislocation" (Alexander, 2008, p. 241). While this may be true of many of the destructive ideas apparent in today's society, it is especially true for the drug war. Part of its persistence has been its ability to appeal to our fears, but its role as the dominant story is now coming to a close.

SO WHAT COMES NEXT?

A compassionate drug policy is an evidence-based policy, recognising that addiction is a sign of underlying needs that require a response from health and social groups, rather than from law enforcement. Legalisation may be a prerequisite for reducing the stigma around drug use and addiction, as criminal behaviour by its definition brings social disapproval. In many ways, reducing addictive behaviours more generally requires investment in many social and health care settings, when we consider what we know about how addiction develops. Stepping back and taking a broad view, there are some points that would help to prevent the development of and curtail the spread of addiction. This is not an exhaustive list by any means, but I have included it as a way of continuing the conversation, and to provide some sources to explore:

1 The earliest addiction prevention is about supporting infants and young children to develop healthy attachments, which happens in the context of nurturing and attuned relationships with their

parents, most often their mothers. Sometimes, families need help to provide this, and a number of effective approaches have been developed, which seek to support mothers to attune to their babies, improving secure attachment and the development of psychological resilience (e.g. Barlow et al., 2008; Olds et al., 1997).

2 Adolescence is a time of particular risk for those with access to substances, and many of those who end up in drug and alcohol treatment services started using in early adolescence or before. Drug education needs to be realistic and respectful, providing information and promoting the ability to make informed choices about drug use. Information alone, and most mass media campaigns bemoaning the unrealistic horrors of drug use are not effective, and can make the situation worse (e.g. UKDPC, 2012).
3 There are promising interventions that can be used with those young people who may have traits that could predispose them to addictive behaviours. An approach called Preventure identifies these traits, and uses cognitive behavioural techniques to support young people to manage their own behaviour, and has been shown to reduce binge drinking, as well as depression, panic and impulsive behaviour. It has had excellent results in both Canada and the UK (Conrod et al., 2013).
4 The majority of people experiencing addictive behaviours will never need a specialist service, unless they are socially isolated or have fewer resources. The first tier of support will be from the community, and if social support is lacking from someone's immediate network, self-help groups and the 12-step fellowships may be vital. It is hoped that the information within this book about different self-help approaches and their pros and cons will support people to make informed decisions, and find or build social networks of recovery.
5 For those that do need more specialist support, the most effective treatment will be based on a respectful and compassionate approach that ensures that personal agency and choice is upheld as far as possible. Physical health, mental health and social care services,

as well as the voluntary sector services supporting them, need appropriate levels of funding, trained staff and systems of governance that advocate and support this. Those serving deprived areas will need increased resources, reflecting the greater needs of the populations they serve.

6 For each of us, understanding that our brains can be 'tricky', that we sometimes have different parts of ourselves that conflict with each other, and recognising the ways that addictive behaviours can develop, can support us to make more informed choices about what we really need from moment to moment. More information about some of the approaches described in Chapters 4 and 5 is included in the reading list at the end of this book.

7 We know that economic inequality contributes to the rise of addiction and poor mental health, so policies promoting equality would likely see a reduction in a range of difficulties (for examples, see the work of the Equality Trust[2]). We are not born equal, and addressing some of the societal and health inequalities around us doesn't just benefit those with the most apparent need, but benefits us all.

We all tell ourselves stories that define who we are and where we have come from. Addiction isn't a weakness, or a moral disorder, but a learned adaptation to distress, isolation or dislocation, and one that each one of us might have faced if our own circumstances had aligned in a particular way. For those that struggle with addictive behaviours, it's not your fault, but it is your responsibility. You don't need to work out how to change on your own, unless that's what works for you, but change is possible, and remember that recovery, or continued growth, is more common than you think. And it can lead you to surpass yourself. There is research that shows that some people who have learned to control their addictive tendencies have higher than average brain growth in areas involved with behavioural control and regulation, as well as higher scores than the general public on measures of quality of life and self-esteem (Connolly et al., 2013; Hibbert and Best, 2011). Recovery from addiction doesn't just make you well, but "better than well" (Best and Lubman, 2012). We might not be able to control the lives we are born into, but we can learn to control our 'tricky brains' and their sometimes destructive tendencies, with compassion for ourselves and our flaws, connection with others, and a commitment to work towards a society that enables us all to reach our full potential.

FURTHER READING

These authors have combined personal experience of addictive behaviours with their considerable professional expertise:

- For an insightful perspective of 'addiction as disordered learning' using the author's developmental history, read *Unbroken Brain: A Revolutionary New Way of Understanding Addiction* by Maia Szalavitz (2016; New York: St Martin's Press).
- For a personal account of addiction from a neuroscientific perspective, read *Memoirs of an Addicted Brain: A Neuroscientist Examines His Former Life on Drugs* by Marc Lewis (2011; New York: PublicAffairs).
- For a vivid and compassionate physician's eye view of addictive behaviours, with a particular emphasis on the influence of early life trauma, read *In the Realm of the Hungry Ghosts: Close Encounters With Addiction* by Gabor Maté (2010; Berkeley: North Atlantic Books).

Books about social influences (and solutions) for addiction:

- For a readable and expansive view, read *The Globalization of Addiction: A Study in Poverty of the Spirit* by Bruce Alexander (2008; Oxford: Oxford University Press).
- The story of Bruce Alexander and his team's work on 'Rat Park' has been re-told many times. A wonderful visual example is by

the Australian comic artist Stuart McMillen, available here: www.stuartmcmillen.com/comic/rat-park/.

- For a far-reaching account of addictive behaviours and disempowerment, read *Power, Powerlessness and Addiction* by Jim Orford (2013; Cambridge: Cambridge University Press).

Books about addiction as choice or learning:

- For a thoughtful account of the neuroscience behind addiction and how this supports a view of addiction as 'deep learning', read *The Biology of Desire: Why Addiction Is Not a Disease* by Marc Lewis (2015; London: PublicAffairs). His blog and discussion pages also offer insightful debate and discussion, and are well worth a read: www.memoirsofanaddictedbrain.com/blog/.
- For a personal account of this relationship from a neuroscientific perspective, read *High Price: A Neuroscientist's Journey of Self-Discovery That Challenges Everything You Know About Drugs and Society* by Carl Hart (2013; London: Penguin Books).

Books about addictive behaviours and psychological interventions (see also References):

- For a step-by-step guide to using mindfulness meditation to overcome addictive behaviours, read *Eight Step Recovery: Using the Buddha's Teachings to Overcome Addiction* by Valerie Mason-John and Paramabandhu Groves (2013; Cambridge: Windhorse).
- See also *Mindfulness-Based Relapse Prevention for Addictive Behaviours* by Sarah Bowen, Neha Chawla and G. Alan Marlatt (2011; New York: Guilford Press), and their associated website, which includes audio exercises, available here: www.mindfulrp.com/default.html.
- For a self-help manual covering some of the techniques outlined in this book, see *The Addiction Recovery Skills Workbook* by Suzette Glasner-Edwards (2015; Oakland, CA: New Harbinger Publications).
- The idea of our 'tricky brains' comes from the work of Professor Paul Gilbert and his research team. See for example his book *The Compassionate Mind* (2009; London: Constable & Robinson), and

the work of the Compassionate Mind Foundation, available here: https://compassionatemind.co.uk/.

Reading about drug policy and its consequences:

- For an urgent and passionate call to end the War on Drugs, read *Chasing the Scream: The First and Last Days of the War on Drugs* by Johann Hari (2015; London: Bloomsbury).
- For a scientific and sensible look at drugs and their consequences, read *Drugs Without the Hot Air: Minimising the Harms of Legal and Illegal Drugs* by David Nutt (2012; Cambridge: UIT Cambridge).

For a random pick of classic novels about addiction, try:

- *Infinite Jest* by David Foster Wallace (1996; New York: Little, Brown).
- *Choke* by Chuck Palahniuk (2001; New York: Anchor Books).
- *Wasted: Coming Back From an Addiction to Starvation* by Marya Hornbacher (1998; London: Flamingo).

NOTES

CHAPTER 4

1 The idea of the 'wise and compassionate companion' comes from Deborah Lee's concept of the 'perfect nurturer'. For example, see: Lee, D. A. (2005). The perfect nurturer: Using imagery to develop compassion within the context of cognitive therapy. In: P. Gilbert (Ed.) *Compassion: Conceptualisations, Research and Use in Psychotherapy*. London: Brunner-Routledge.

CHAPTER 5

1 For more information on the relationship between income inequality and a wide range of health, social and economic consequences, see the work of the Equality Trust at: www.equalitytrust.org.uk/.

CHAPTER 6

1 Retrieved from Transform Drug Policy Foundation at: www.tdpf.org.uk/resources/legal-regulation on 13 August 2017.
2 www.equalitytrust.org.uk/.

REFERENCES

ACMD. (2011). *Hidden Harm*. London: Advisory Council on the Misuse of Drugs Alcoholics.

Alcoholics Anonymous UK. (2017). *About Alcoholism*. [Online]. [Accessed 11 August 2017]. Available from: www.alcoholics-anonymous.org.uk/About-AA/Newcomers/About-Alcoholism.

Alexander, B. K. (2008). *The Globalization of Addiction: A Study in Poverty of the Spirit*. Oxford: Oxford University Press.

Alexander, B. K., Coambs, R. B. and Hadaway, P. F. (1978). The effect of housing and gender on morphine self-administration in rats. *Psychopharmacology*, **58**(2), pp. 175–179.

American Psychiatric Association. (2013). *Diagnostic and Statistical Manual of Mental Disorders*. 5th ed. Washington, DC: American Psychiatric Association.

AMRC. (2013). *Measuring Up: The Medical Profession's Prescription for the Nation's Obesity Crisis*. London: Academy of Medical Royal Colleges.

Anda, R. F., Felitti, V. J., Walker, J., Whitfield, C. L., Bremner, J. D., Perry, B. D., Dube, S. R. and Giles, W. H. (2006). The enduring effects of abuse and related adverse experiences in childhood: A convergence of evidence from neurobiology and epidemiology. *European Archives of Psychiatry and Clinical Neuroscience*, **56**(3), pp. 174–186.

Anonymous. (2001). *The Big Book*. 4th ed. Alcoholics Anonymous World Services, Inc. Available from: www.aa.org/pages/en_US/alcoholics-anonymous.

ASH. (2017). *Key Dates in the History of Anti-Tobacco Campaigning*. London: Action on Smoking and Health.

Baggini, J. (2015). Do your genes determine your entire life? *Guardian*. [Online]. 19 March. [Accessed 11 August 2017]. Available from: www.theguardian.com/science/2015/mar/19/do-your-genes-determine-your-entire-life.

Bandele, A. (2016). Jay-Z: The war on drugs is an epic fail. *New York Times*. [Online]. 15 September 2016. [Accessed 10 August 2017]. Available from: www.nytimes.com/2016/09/15/opinion/jay-z-the-war-on-drugs-is-an-epic-fail.html.

Bandura, A. (1977). Self-efficacy: Toward a unifying theory of behavioural change. *Psychological Review*, **84**(2), pp. 191–215.

Barlow, J., McMillan, A. S., Kirkpatrick, S., Ghate, D., Smith, M. and Barnes, J. (2008). *Health-Led Parenting Interventions in Pregnancy and Early Years*. London: Department for Children, Schools and Families.

Bauld, L., Bell, K., McCullough, L., Richardson, L. and Greaves, L. (2009). The effectiveness of NHS smoking cessation services: A systematic review. *Journal of Public Health*, **32**(1), pp. 71–82.

Baumeister, R. F., Bratslavsky, E., Muraven, M. and Tice, D. M. (1998). Ego depletion: Is the active self a limited resource? *Journal of Personality and Social Psychology*, **74**(5), pp. 1252–1265.

BBC Health. (2012). 'Binge-drinking gene' discovered. *BBC*. [Online]. 4 December. [Accessed 11 August 2017]. Available from: www.bbc.co.uk/news/health-20583113.

Bellis, M., Lowey, H., Leckenby, N., Hughes, K. and Harrison, D. (2014). Adverse childhood experiences: Retrospective study to determine their impact on adult health behaviours and health outcomes in a UK population. *Journal of Public Health*, **36**(1), pp. 81–91.

Bem, D. J. (1972). Self-perception theory. *Advances in Experimental Social Psychology*, **6**, pp. 1–62.

Berridge, K. and Kringelbach, M. L. (2008). Affective neuroscience of pleasure: Reward in humans and animals. *Psychopharmacology*, **199**, pp. 457–480.

Berridge, K. and Robinson, T. E. (2016). Liking, wanting and the incentive-sensitization theory of addiction. *American Psychologist*, **71**(8), pp. 670–679.

Best, D. W. and Lubman, D. I. (2012). The recovery paradigm: A model of hope and change for alcohol and drug addiction. *Australian Family Physician*, **41**(8), pp. 593–597.

Bowden, C. (2011). *Murder City: Ciudad Juarez and the Global Economy's New Killing Fields*. New York: Nation Books. Cited in Hari, J. (2015). *Chasing the Scream: The First and Last Days of the War on Drugs*. London: Bloomsbury.

Bowlby, J. (1969). *Attachment. Attachment and Loss: Vol. 1. Loss*. New York: Basic Books.

Breen, R. B. and Zimmerman, M. (2002). Rapid onset of pathological gambling in machine gamblers. *Journal of Gambling Studies*, **18**(1), pp. 31–43.

Brion, M., Pitel, A.-L., Beaunieux, H. and Maurage, P. (2014). Revisiting the continuum hypothesis: Toward in an-depth exploration of executive functions in Korsakoff Syndrome. *Frontiers in Human Neuroscience*, **8**(498), pp. 1–7.

Broks, P. (2003). *Into the Silent Land: Travels in Neuropsychology*. New York: Atlantic Books.

Brooks, P. J., Enoch, M.-A., Goldman, D., Li, T.-K. and Yokoyama, A. (2009). The alcohol flushing response: An unrecognised risk for esophageal cancer from alcohol consumption. *PLOS Medicine*, **6**(3), pp. e1000050.

Buchman, D. Z. and Reiner, P. (2010). Stigma and addiction: Being and becoming. *American Journal of Bioethics*, **9**(9), pp. 18–19.

CASA. (2011). *Adolescent Substance Use: America's #1 Public Health Problem*. New York: National Center on Addiction and Substance Abuse. [Online]. [Accessed 11 August 2017]. Available from: www.centeronaddiction.org/addiction-research/reports/adolescent-substance-use-america%E2%80%99s-1-public-health-problem.

CDC. (2011). *Drug Poisoning Deaths in the United States, 1980–2008: NCHS Data Brief No. 81*. Atlanta: Centers for Disease Control and Prevention.

Chandler, M. J. and Lalonde, C. E. (2008). Cultural continuity as a protective factor against suicide in first nations youth. *Horizons: A Special Issue on Aboriginal Youth, Hope or Heartbreak: Aboriginal Youth and Canada's Future*, **10**(1), pp. 68–72.

Clinical Guidelines on Drug Misuse and Dependence Update, Independent Expert Working Group. (2017). *Drug Misuse and Dependence: UK Guidelines on Clinical Management*. London: Department of Health.

Connolly, C. G., Bell, R. P., Foxe, J. J. and Garavan, H. (2013). Dissociated grey matter changes with prolonged addiction and extended abstinence in cocaine users. *PLOS ONE*, **8**(3), e59645.

Conrod, P. J., O'Leary-Barrett, M., Newton, N., Topper, L., Castellanos-Ryan, N., Mackie, C. and Girard, A. (2013). Effectiveness of a selective, personality-targeted prevention program for adolescent alcohol use and misuse: A cluster randomized controlled trial. *JAMA Psychiatry*, **70**(3), pp. 334–342.

Copello, A., Orford, J., Hodgson, R., Tober, G. and Barrett, C. on behalf of the UKATT Research Team. (2002). Social behaviour and network therapy: Basic principles and early experiences. *Addictive Behaviours*, **27**(3), pp. 345–366.

Copello, A., Templeton, L., Orford, J. and Velleman, R. (2010). The 5-step method: Principles and practice. *Drugs: Education, Prevention and Policy* **17**, pp. 86–99.

Corrigan, J. D., Rust, E. and Lamb-Hart, G. L. (1995). The nature and extent of substance abuse problems among persons with traumatic brain injuries. *Journal of Head Trauma Rehabilitation*, **10**(3), pp. 29–45.

Crittenden, P. M. and DiLalla, D. L. (1988). Compulsive compliance: The development of an inhibitory coping strategy in infancy. *Journal of Abnormal Child Psychology*, **16**(5), pp. 585–599.

Dawson, D. A., Grant, B. F., Stinson, F. S., Chou, P. S., Huang, B. and Ruan, W. J. (2005). Recovery from DSM-IV alcohol dependence: United States, 2001–2002. *Addiction*, **100**, pp. 281–292.

Dillon, P. (2002). *The Much-Lamented Death of Madam Geneva: The Eighteenth-Century Gin Craze*. London: Review.

Eastwood, N., Shiner, M. and Bear, D. (2013). *The Numbers in Black and White: Ethnic Disparities in the Policing and Prosecution of Drug Offences in England and Wales*. London: Release Publication. [Online]. [Accessed 11 August 2017]. Available from: www.release.org.uk/publications/numbers-black-and-white-ethnic-disparities-policing-and-prosecution-drug-offences.

EMCDDA. (2017a). *European Drug Report: Trends and Developments*. Luxembourg: European Monitoring Centre for Drugs and Drug Addiction.

EMCDDA. (2017b). *UK Country Drug Report*. Luxembourg: European Monitoring Centre for Drugs and Drug Addiction.

Everitt, B. J. and Robbins, T. W. (2013). From the ventral to the dorsal striatum: Devolving views of their role in drug addiction. *Neuroscience and Biobehavioural Reviews*, **37**(9A), pp. 1946–1954.

FADA. (2013). *The Impact of Substance Abuse on the Child Welfare System*. Florida Alcohol and Drug Abuse Association. [Online]. [Accessed 13 August 2017]. Available from: www.fadaa.org/documents/Legislative%20Booklets/ChildWelfare.pdf.

Felitti, V. J. (2004). The origins of addiction: Evidence from the Adverse Childhood Experiences Study. *Praxis der Kinderpsychologie und Kinderpsychiatrie*, **52**(8), pp. 547–559.

Fernandez-Serrano, M. J., Perez-Garcia, M. and Verdejo-Garcia, A. (2011). What are the specific vs. generalised effects of drugs of abuse on neuropsychological performance? *Neuroscience and Biobehavioural Reviews*, **35**, pp. 377–406.

Ferri, M., Amato, L. and Davoli, M. (2006). Alcoholics Anonymous and other 12-step programmes for alcohol dependence. *Cochrane Database of Systematic Reviews*, Issue 3.

Foster, J. (2000). Social exclusion, crime and drugs. *Drugs: Education, Prevention and Policy*, **7**(4), pp. 317–330.

Galea, S. and Vlakov, D. (2002). Social determinants and the health of drug users: Socioeconomic status, homelessness and incarceration. *Public Health Reports*, **117**(1), pp. S135–S145.

Gander, K. (2014). Being lazy could be genetic say scientists. *Independent*. 14 February. [Accessed 11 August 2017]. Available from: www.independent.co.uk/news/science/being-lazy-could-be-genetic-say-scientists-9128595.

Gielen, N., Havermans, R. C., Tekelenburg, M. and Jansen, A. (2012). Prevalence of post-traumatic stress disorder among patients with substance use disorder: It is higher than clinicians think it is. *European Journal of Psychotraumatology*, **3**(17734), pp. 1–9.

Goldstein, R. Z. and Volkow, N. D. (2011). Dysfunction of the prefrontal cortex in addiction: Neuroimaging findings and clinical implications. *Nature Reviews Neuroscience*, **12**, pp. 652–669.

Gutteridge, N. (2015). Unbe-cheese-able! Shock as scientists say cheese is as addictive as CRACK COCAINE. *Express*. [Online]. [Accessed 11 August 2017]. Available from: www.express.co.uk/news/science/614192/Scientists-cheese-addictive-crack-cocaine-dairy-study obesity-crisis.

Guttmannova, K., Lee, C. M., Kilmer, J. R., Fleming, C. B., Rhew, I. C., Kosterman, R. and Larimer, M. E. (2016). Impacts of changing marijuana policies on alcohol use in the United States. *Alcoholism: Clinical and Experimental Research*, **40**(1), pp. 33–46.

Hari, J. (2015). *Chasing the Scream: The First and Last Days of the War on Drugs*. London: Bloomsbury.

Hart, C. (2013a). *High Price: A Neuroscientist's Journey of Self-Discovery that Challenges Everything You Know About Drugs and Society*. London: Penguin Books.

Hart, C. (2013b). *High Price: Drugs, Neuroscience and Discovering Myself*. London: Penguin Books.

Hartogsohn, I. (2016). Set and setting, psychedelics and the placebo response: An extra-pharmacological perspective on psychopharmacology. *Journal of Psychopharmacology*, **30**(12), pp. 1259–1267.

Hartogsohn, I. (2017). Constructing drug effects: A history of set and setting. *Drug Science, Policy and Law*, **3**, pp. 1–17.

Hawkes, N. (2011). Highs and lows of drug decriminalisation. *British Medical Journal*, **343**, d6881.

Heath, D. B. (1998). Cultural variations among drinking patterns. In: M. Grant and J. Litvak, eds. *Drinking Patterns and their Consequences*. Washington, DC: Taylor & Francis.

Heather, N. (2017). On defining addiction. In: N. Heather and G. Segal, eds. *Addiction and Choice: Rethinking the Relationship*. Oxford: Oxford University Press.

Hebb, D. (1949). *The Organization of Behavior*. New York: Wiley & Sons.

Heyman, G. M. (2013). Addiction and choice: Theory and new data. *Frontiers in Psychiatry*, **4**, pp. 1–5.

Hibbert, L. and Best, D. (2011). Assessing recovery and functioning in former problem drinkers at different stages of their recovery journeys. *Drug and Alcohol Review*, **30**, pp. 12–20.

Home Office. (2014). *Drugs: International Comparators*. London: Home Office.

Home Office. (2015). *Drug Misuse: Findings From the 2014/2015 Crime Survey for England and Wales*. 2nd ed. London: Home Office.

Human Rights Watch. (2009). *Decades of Disparity: Drug Arrests and Race in the United States*. [Online]. [Accessed 11 August 2017]. Available from: www.hrw.org/sites/default/files/reports/us0309web_1.pdf.

Kellerman, N. P. (2013). Epigenetic transmission of Holocaust trauma: Can nightmares be inherited? *Israel Journal of Psychiatry and Related Sciences*, **50**(1), pp. 33–39.

Kellogg, S. H. (2003). On 'Gradualism' and the building of the harm reduction-abstinence continuum. *Journal of Substance Abuse Treatment*, **25**, pp. 241–247.

Kellogg, S. H. (2016). Addiction Treatment should be the work of liberation – But what does such a model look like? *Influence*. [Online]. 24 August. [Accessed 9 August 2017]. Available from: http://theinfluence.org/addiction-treatment-should-be-the-work-of-liberation-but-what-does-such-a-model-look-like/.

Khantzian, E. J. (1985). The self-medication hypothesis of addictive disorders: Focus on heroin and cocaine dependence. *American Journal of Psychiatry*, **142**(11), pp. 1259–1264.

Kine, P. (2017). *The Philippines' Duterte Incites Vigilante Violence*. New York: Human Rights Watch. [Online]. [Accessed 11 August 2017]. Available from: www.hrw.org/news/2017/04/19/philippines-duterte-incites-vigilante-violence.

Kopelman, M. D., Thomson, A., Guerrini, I. and Marshall, E. J. (2009). The Korsakoff Syndrome: Clinical aspects, psychology and treatment. *Alcohol & Alcoholism*, **44**(2), pp. 148–154.

Kroll, D. (2003). Living with an elephant: Growing up with parental substance misuse. *Child and Family Social Work*, **9**, pp. 129–140.

Lambie, I. and Randell, I. (2013). The impact of incarceration on juvenile offenders. *Clinical Psychology Review*, **33**, pp. 448–459.

Larimer, M. E. (2015). Impacts of changing marijuana policies on alcohol use in the United States. *Alcoholism: Clinical and Experimental Research*, **40**(1), pp. 33–46.

Lewis, M. (2015). *The Biology of Desire: Why Addiction Is Not a Disease*. London: Scribe.

Litt, M., Kadden, R., Kabela-Cormier, E. and Petry, N. (2007). Changing network support for drinking: Initial findings from the network support project. *Journal of Consulting and Clinical Psychology*, **75**, pp. 542–555.

Lopez-Quintero, C., Hasin, D. H., de los Cobos, J. P., Pines, A., Want, S., Grant, B. F. and Blanco, C. (2011). Probability and predictors of remission from lifetime nicotine, alcohol, cannabis or cocaine dependence: Results from the National Epidemiologic Survey on Alcohol and Related Conditions. *Addiction*, **106**(3), pp. 657–669.

Luby, J., Belden, A., Botteron, K., Marrus, N., Harms, M. P., Babb, C., Nishino, T. and Barch, D. (2013). The effects of poverty on childhood brain development: The mediating effect of caregiving and stressful life events. *JAMA Pediatrics*, **167**(12), pp. 1135–1142.

Manning, V., Best, D. W., Faulkner, N. and Titherington, E. (2009). New estimates of the number of children living with substance misusing parents: Results from UK national household surveys. *Biomed Central Public Health*, **9**, p. 377.

Marlatt, G. A. (2002). Buddhist philosophy and the treatment of addictive behaviour. *Cognitive and Behavioural Practice*, **9**, pp. 44–50.

Marmot, M. G. (2006). Status Syndrome: A challenge to medicine. *JAMA*, **295**(11), pp. 1304–1307.

Maslow, A. H. (1943). A theory of human motivation. *Psychological Review*, **50**(4), pp. 370–396.

Masson, J. M., ed. (1985). *The Complete Letters of Sigmund Freud to Wilhelm Fliess, 1887–1904*. Cambridge: Harvard University Press. Quote taken from Freud's letter to Wilhelm Fleiss, 22 December 1897. [Excerpts online]. [Accessed 23 October 2016]. Available from: www3.haverford.edu/psychology/ddavis/ffliess.html.

Maté, G. (2010). *In the Realm of Hungry Ghosts: Close Encounters With Addiction*. Berkeley, CA: North Atlantic Books.

Meyers, R. J., Miller, W. R., Hill, D. E. and Tonigan, J. S. (1999). Community Reinforcement and Family Training (CRAFT): Engaging unmotivated drug users in treatment. *Journal of Substance Abuse*, **10**(3), pp. 291–308.

Michalak, L., Trocki, K. and Bond, J. (2007). Religion and alcohol in the US National Alcohol Survey: How important is religion for abstention and drinking? *Drug and Alcohol Dependence*, **87**(2–3), pp. 268–280.

Miller, W. R. and Rollnick, S. (2013). *Motivational Interviewing: Helping People Change*. 3rd ed. New York: Guilford Press.

Miron, J. (1999). *Violence and US Prohibitions of Drugs and Alcohol*. Cambridge: National Bureau of Economic Research. [Online]. [Accessed 13 August 2017]. Available from: www.nber.org/papers/w6950.pdf.

Mischel, W., Shoda, Y. and Rodriguez, M. L. (1989). Delay of gratification in children. *Science*, **244**(4907), pp. 933–938.

Mitcheson, L., Maslin, J., Meynen, T., Morrison, T., Hill, R. and Wanigaratne, S. (2010). *Applied Cognitive and Behavioural Approaches to the Treatment of Addiction*. West Sussex: John Wiley & Sons.

Musto, D. (1999). *The American Disease: Origins of Narcotics Control*. Oxford: Oxford University Press.

Nevis, E. C., ed. (2000). *Gestalt Therapy: Perspectives and Applications*. Cambridge, MA: GestaltPress.

NTA. (2010). *Psychosocial Interventions for Drug Misuse*. London: National Treatment Agency.

Nutt, D., King, L. A. and Phillips, L. D. on behalf of the Independent Scientific Committee on Drugs. (2010). Drug harms in the UK: A multicriterion decision analysis. *Lancet*, **376**(9752), pp. 1558–1565.

Olds, D. L., Eckenrode, J., Henderson, C. R., Kitzman, H., Powers, J., Cole, R., Sidora, K., Morris, P., Pettitt, L. M. and Luckey, D. (1997). Long-term effects of home visitation on maternal life course and child abuse and neglect. Fifteen-year follow-up of a randomized trial. *JAMA: The Journal of the American Medical Association*, **278**(8), pp. 637–643.

ONS. (2016). *Smoking Habits in the UK*. London: Office for National Statistics.

Orford, J., Copello, A., Velleman, R. and Templeton, L. (2010). Family members affected by a close relative's addiction: The stress-strain-coping-support model. *Drugs: Education, Prevention and Policy*, **17**(Supplement 1), pp. 36–43.

Orford, J., Velleman, R., Natera, G., Templeton, L. and Copello, A. (2013). Addiction in the family is a major but neglected contributor to the global burden of adult ill-health. *Social Science and Medicine*, **78**, pp. 70–77.

Peele, S., Brodsky, A. and Arnold, M. (1992). *The Truth About Addiction and Recovery*. New York: Simon & Schuster. [Online]. [Accessed 13 August 2017]. Available from: www.peele.net/lib/truth_1.html.

Petry, N. (2000). A comprehensive guide to the application of contingency management procedures in clinical settings. *Drug and Alcohol Dependence*, **58**, pp. 9–25.

PHE. (2014). *Alcohol and Drugs Prevention, Treatment and Recovery: Why Invest?* London: Public Health England.

Rehm, J., Samokhvalov, A. V. and Shield, K. D. (2013). Global burden of alcoholic liver diseases. *Journal of Hepatology*, **59**(1), pp. 160–168.

Rogers, C. (1961). *On Becoming a Person: A Therapist's View of Psychotherapy*. London: Constable.

Ryan, F. (2013). *Cognitive Therapy for Addiction*. West Sussex: John Wiley & Sons.

Saggers, S. and Gray, D. (1998). *Dealing With Alcohol: Indigenous Usage in Australia, New Zealand and Canada*. Melbourne: Cambridge University Press.

Scottish Government. (2008). *The Road to Recovery*. Edinburgh: Scottish Government.

Seligman, M. (2002). *Authentic Happiness*. New York: Atria Books.

The Sentencing Project. (2013). *Report of the Sentencing Project to the United Nations Human Rights Committee*. Washington, DC: The Sentencing Project. [Online]. [Accessed 14 August 2017]. Available from: www.sentencingproject.org/publications/shadow-report-to-the-united-nations-human-rights-committee-regarding-racial-disparities-in-the-united-states-criminal-justice-system.

Sessa, B. and Nutt, D. (2015). Making a medicine out of MDMA. *British Journal of Psychiatry*, **206**(1), pp. 4–6.

Shaffer, H. (1984). Uber coca: Freud's cocaine discoveries. *Journal of Substance Abuse Treatment*, **1**(3), pp. 205–217.

Shulte, E., Avena, N. M. and Gearhardt, A. N. (2015). Which foods may be addictive? The roles of processing, fat content and glycemic load. *PLOS ONE*, **10**(2), pp. 1–18.

Smith, D. G. and Robbins, T. W. (2013). The neurobiological underpinnings of obesity and binge eating: A rationale for adopting the food addiction model. *Biological Psychiatry*, **73**(9), pp. 804–810.

Smith, J. E., Meyers, R. J. and Miller, W. R. (2001). The Community Reinforcement Approach to the treatment of substance use disorders. *American Journal on Addictions*, **10**(1), pp. 51–59.

Standing, G. (2015). The precariat and class struggle. *Revista Crítica de Ciências Sociais Annual Review*, **7**, pp. 3–16.

Stevens, A. and Hughes, C. E. (2012). A resounding success or a disastrous failure: Re-examining the interpretation of evidence on the Portuguese decriminalisation of illicit drugs. *Drug and Alcohol Review*, **31**(1), pp. 101–113.

Szalavitz, M. (2015). Genetics: No more addictive personality. *Nature*, **522**(7557), pp. 48–49.

Szalavitz, M. (2016). *Unbroken Brain: A Revolutionary New Way of Understanding Addiction*. New York: St Martin's Press.

Szalavitz, M. and Perry, B. (2010). *Born for Love: Why Empathy Is Essential, and Endangered*. New York: HarperCollins.

Tatarsky, A. (2003). Harm reduction psychotherapy: Extending the reach of traditional substance use treatment. *Journal of Substance Abuse Treatment*, **25**, pp. 249–256.

TDPF. (2009) *After the War on Drugs: Blueprint for Regulation*. Bristol: Transform Drug Policy Foundation.

Thich Nhat Han. (2007). *Two Treasures: Buddhist Teachings on Awakening to True Happiness*. Berkeley, CA: Parallax Press.

Treback, A. S., Zeese, K. B. and Friedman, M. (1992). *Friedman and Szasz on Liberty and Drugs: Essays on the Free Market and Prohibition*. Washington, DC: Drug Policy Foundation Press.

UKDPC. (2012). *A Fresh Approach to Drugs*. London: UK Drug Policy Commission. [Online]. [Accessed 23 August 2017]. Available from: www.ukdpc.org.uk/

wp-content/uploads/a-fresh-approach-to-drugs-the-final-report-of-the-uk-drug-policy-commission.pdf.

UK Drug Policy Commission Recovery Consensus Group. (2008). *A Vision of Recovery*. London: UKDPC.

UK Smart Recovery. (2016). Information available from: www.smartrecovery.org.uk.

UNODC. (2015). *World Drug Report*. Vienna: UN Office on Drugs and Crime. [Online]. [Accessed 11 August 2017]. Available from: www.unodc.org/documents/wdr2015/WDR15_Drug_use_health_consequences.pdf.

UNODC. (2016). *World Drug Report*. Vienna: UN Office on Drugs and Crime.

UNODC. (2017). *World Drug Report*. United Nations. [Online]. [Accessed 11 August 2017]. Available from: www.unodc.org/wdr2017/field/Booklet_1_EXSUM.pdf.

Villettaz, P., Gilliéron, G. and Killias, M. (2014). *The Effects on Re-offending of Custodial Versus Non-Custodial Sanctions*. Stockholm: Swedish Council for Crime Prevention.

Waldorf, D. and Biernacki, P. (1981). The natural recovery from opiate addiction: some preliminary findings. *Journal of Drug Issues*, **11**(1), pp. 61–74.

Weaver, T., Madden, P., Charles, V., Stimson, G., Renton, A., Tyrer, P., Barnes, T., Bench, C., Middleton, H., Wright, N., Paterson, S., Shanahan, W., Seivewright, N. and Ford, C. (2003). Comorbidity of substance misuse and mental illness in community mental health and substance misuse services. *British Journal of Psychiatry*, **183**, pp. 304–313.

West, R. and Brown, J. (2013). *Theory of Addiction*. 2nd ed. Oxford: Wiley Blackwell.

White, W. L. (1996). *Pathways: From the Culture of Addiction to the Culture of Recovery*. 2nd ed. Center City, MN: Hazelden.

White, W. L. (2009). Executive summary, peer-based addiction recovery support: History, theory, practice, and scientific evaluation. *Counselor*, **10**(5), pp. 54–59.

White, W. L. and Cloud, W. (2008). Recovery capital: A primer for addictions professionals. *Counselor*, **9**(5), pp. 22–27.

WHO. (1992). *The ICD-10 Classification of Mental and Behavioural Disorders: Clinical Descriptions and Diagnostic Guidelines*. Geneva: World Health Organization.

WHO. (2014). *Global Status Report on Alcohol and Health*. Geneva: World Health Organization.

WHO/UN Joint Statement. (2017). *Joint United Nations Statement on Ending Discrimination in Health Care Settings*. 27th June. World Health Organization/United Nations. [Online]. [Accessed 13 August 2017]. Available from: www.who.int/mediacentre/news/statements/2017/discrimination-in-health-care/en/.

Wilens, T. E., Faraone, S. V., Biederman, J. and Gunawardene, S. (2003). Does stimulant therapy of attention-deficit/hyperactivity disorder beget later substance abuse? A meta-analytic review of the literature. *Pediatrics*, **111**, pp. 179–185.

Witkiewitz, K. and Marlatt, G. A. (2004). Relapse prevention for alcohol and drug problems: That was Zen, this is Tao. *American Psychologist*, **59**(4), pp. 224–235.

Wodak, A. (1994). Olympian ideas or pragmatism. *Addiction*, **89**, pp. 803–804.

Young, J., Klosko, J. and Weishaar, M. E. (2003). *Schema Therapy: A Practitioner's Guide*. New York: Guilford Press.

Zernig, G., Kummer, K. K. and Prast, J. M. (2013). Dyadic social interaction as an alternative reward to cocaine. *Frontiers in Psychiatry*, **4**(100), pp. 1–5.

Zinberg, N. E. (1984). *Drug, Set and Setting: The Basis for Controlled Intoxicant Use*. New Haven, CT: Yale University Press.

Zubrick, S. R., Lawrence, D., Silburn, S. R., Blair, E., Milroy, H., Wilkes, T., Eades, S., D'Antoine, H., Read, A., Ishiguchi, P. and Doyle, S. (2004). *The Western Australian Aboriginal Child Health Survey: The Health of Aboriginal Children and Young People*. vol. 1. Perth: Telethon Institute for Child Health Research.

Printed in the United States
by Baker & Taylor Publisher Services